THIS BOOK
BELONGS TO:

_____

Praise for *WHEN STRIVINGS CEASE*

"In Ruth's personal and generous way, she has crafted the message that busy and driven Christians need to hear: no amount of self-improvement or the world's approval could ever replace our need for God's amazing grace. This is a book for us all."

—LYSA TERKEURST, #1 *NEW YORK TIMES* BESTSELLING AUTHOR AND PRESIDENT OF PROVERBS 31 MINISTRIES

"In *When Strivings Cease*, Ruth Chou Simons paints beautiful pictures with words—pictures of shame and inadequacy that we see ourselves in, and a picture of the rest we long to find ourselves in. Ruth's humor, vulnerability, scriptural insight, and friendly offer of gospel grace come through on every page."

—NANCY GUTHRIE, AUTHOR AND BIBLE TEACHER

"If you are a recovering people pleaser, if you're tired of striving and measuring up, *When Strivings Cease* will be like water to your soul."

—JENNIE ALLEN, *NEW YORK TIMES* BESTSELLING AUTHOR OF *GET OUT OF YOUR HEAD* AND FOUNDER AND VISIONARY OF IF:GATHERING

"Masterfully written with honest prose, compelling story-telling, and clear Bible teaching, Ruth communicates the message of the gospel as she invites us to leave behind the false hope of self-improvement and walk in the fullness of God's grace through Christ."

—GRETCHEN SAFFLES, BESTSELLING AUTHOR OF *THE WELL-WATERED WOMAN* AND FOUNDER OF WELL-WATERED WOMEN

"Ruth invites us into an understanding of how grace shapes the Christ-follower through both surrender and growth. These are not theological abstractions for her, but hard-won truths born from her own tenderly told story."

—JEN WILKIN, AUTHOR AND BIBLE TEACHER

"Ruth Chou Simons firmly but gently redirects us back to Scripture as the primary source on what it means to trust the lifesaving, life-changing grace of Jesus. This book will resonate with any Christian who has ever wondered if they measure up to the gospel they profess to believe."

—AMANDA BIBLE WILLIAMS AND RAECHEL MYERS, COFOUNDERS OF SHE READS TRUTH AND EDITORS OF THE *SHE READS TRUTH BIBLE*

"I've had the great honor of being in Ruth's physical presence—her faith, her trust, and her reliance on the goodness of God literally makes you feel differently than you did before you encountered her. She is a woman who knows the depths of grace and freedom. You will love this book. It will change your life."

—JESS CONNOLLY, AUTHOR OF *YOU ARE THE GIRL FOR THE JOB* AND *BREAKING FREE FROM BODY SHAME*

"Written with compassion, honesty, humility, and biblical wisdom, it's clear Ruth understands the demands women experience, as well as the pressure we put on ourselves. This book is a needed (and welcome) word of refreshment, reminding us of who God is and what he has already accomplished for us in Christ."

—MELISSA KRUGER, AUTHOR AND DIRECTOR OF WOMEN'S INITIATIVES FOR THE GOSPEL COALITION

"I can't think of a more timely word than the timeless truth that Jesus, alone, is enough—for our inadequacies, insecurities, hopes, and dreams. I love how my sister, Ruth Chou Simons, helps us trade our striving for security in God's grace in these pages. If you are weary and unable to simply try harder anymore, this book is for you."

—LISA WHITTLE, BIBLE TEACHER, PODCAST HOST, AND BESTSELLING AUTHOR OF *JESUS OVER EVERYTHING*

"There are only a few people in this world where their words immediately flood my heart and mind with peace and truth and grace all at the same time. Ruth is one of those people for my wife and me! This book is a must-read for anyone dealing with the temptations of a frantic and busy and difficult world—also known as all of us!"

—JEFFERSON BETHKE, *NEW YORK TIMES* BESTSELLING AUTHOR

"In a world of self-improvement and self-help, Ruth Simons delivers the message we all need to hear: We're saved by grace, and we grow by grace. With relatability, raw honesty, and kindness, Ruth provides a clear call to women, pointing them to their only true hope in the saving work of Jesus Christ."

—EMILY JENSEN AND LAURA WIFLER,
COFOUNDERS OF RISEN MOTHERHOOD

"*When Strivings Cease* is a breath of fresh air. Ruth is not only a wonderful storyteller, but she is remarkably open about her own journey and struggle with performing for God. I could relate to her experience on so many levels and appreciate the focus on God's grace and sufficiency."

—SEAN MCDOWELL, PHD, BIOLA UNIVERSITY
PROFESSOR, SPEAKER, YOUTUBER, AND AUTHOR

"As someone who easily reverts to earning my way in the world, *When Strivings Cease* turned my eyes back to the heart of the gospel. The way has been earned; we just have to accept it. Ruth's willingness to offer up her life story to illustrate the power of trusting God's grace blesses all who read her words with an open heart."

—PHYLICIA MASONHEIMER, AUTHOR AND FOUNDER
OF EVERY WOMAN A THEOLOGIAN

"In *When Strivings Cease*, Ruth has revealed 'the gospel of self-improvement' for what it truly is—a works-based gospel which, of course, is no gospel at all. What's the alternative? Moving from a knowledge of God's grace to an experience of it. That's what Ruth helps you do in this excellent book."

—JORDAN RAYNOR, NATIONAL BESTSELLING AUTHOR
OF *CALLED TO CREATE* AND *MASTER OF ONE*

"As I turned the pages of *When Strivings Cease*, the word *freedom* repeated in my head like a mantra—Ruth is marching us toward freedom in Christ. Through biblical teaching and vulnerability, Ruth helps us understand grace and the real Jesus we all long to know. I'll be returning to this book for years to come, and so will you."

—TRILLIA NEWBELL, AUTHOR OF *GOD'S VERY GOOD
IDEA*, *SACRED ENDURANCE*, AND *IF GOD IS FOR US*

"Ruth is a trusted author, friend, and artist who uses her gifts to display the truth of God's favor and grace in our lives. She models a beautiful tension of stewardship and surrender. This is a must-read!"

—REBEKAH LYONS, BESTSELLING AUTHOR OF
RHYTHMS OF RENEWAL AND *YOU ARE FREE*

"In a world that screams do more, run faster, build more, get more attractive, find more followers, be more successful, Ruth is gently reminding us that we are already enough because of Jesus. You will be encouraged and changed when you close the last page."

—JAMIE IVEY, BESTSELLING AUTHOR AND HOST OF
THE HAPPY HOUR WITH JAMIE IVEY PODCAST

"A timeless, relatable, and vulnerable read about tvrading the myth of the American dream for freedom found in the kingdom of Heaven."

—MYQUILLYN SMITH, *NEW YORK TIMES*
BESTSELLING AUTHOR OF *WELCOME HOME*

"As vulnerable as it is funny as it is beautiful. Ruth's story brings the timeless truth of Scripture to our social media moment of striving, 'You can stop performing. God's grace really is enough.'"

—JUSTIN WHITMEL EARLEY, LAWYER AND AUTHOR OF *THE COMMON RULE* AND *HABITS OF THE HOUSEHOLD*

"A blending of her story as an Asian American woman growing up in two worlds along with generous amounts of scripture, Ruth pulls hard-won lessons from her life to redirect our understanding of where we find rest, peace, and intimacy with God."

—VIVIAN MABUNI, SPEAKER, PODCAST HOST, FOUNDER OF SOMEDAY
IS HERE, AND AUTHOR OF *OPEN HANDS, WILLING HEART*

"With clarity and her signature theological depth, Ruth gives us permission to exchange self-reliance for God-reliance. Her eloquent prose and humble spirit shine in this book that will transform the way you see God's grace for you."

—TIMOTHY D. WILLARD, PhD, C. S. LEWIS SCHOLAR,
AND AUTHOR OF *WHERE BEAUTY BEGINS*

WHEN STRIVINGS CEASE

REPLACING THE GOSPEL OF SELF-IMPROVEMENT WITH
THE GOSPEL OF LIFE-TRANSFORMING GRACE

RUTH CHOU SIMONS

NELSON
BOOKS

An Imprint of Thomas Nelson

Published in Nashville, Tennessee, by Nelson Books, an imprint of Thomas Nelson. Nelson Books and Thomas Nelson are registered trademarks of HarperCollins Christian Publishing, Inc.

Published in association with William K. Jensen Literary Agency, 119 Bampton Court, Eugene, Oregon 97404.

Thomas Nelson titles may be purchased in bulk for educational, business, fundraising, or sales promotional use. For information, please email SpecialMarkets@ThomasNelson.com.

Scripture quotations marked ESV are taken from the ESV® Bible (The Holy Bible, English Standard Version®). Copyright © 2001 by Crossway, a publishing ministry of Good News Publishers. Used by permission. All rights reserved.

Scripture quotations marked NIV are from the Holy Bible, New International Version®, NIV®. Copyright © 1973, 1978, 1984, 2011 by Biblica, Inc.® Used by permission of Zondervan. All rights reserved worldwide. www. zondervan.com The "NIV" and "New International Version" are trademarks registered in the United States Patent and Trademark Office by Biblica, Inc.®

Scripture quotations marked NASB are from the New American Standard Bible® (NASB), Copyright © 1960, 1962, 1963, 1968, 1971, 1972, 1973, 1975, 1977, 1995 by The Lockman Foundation. Used by permission. www.Lockman.org.

Scripture quotations marked AMP are from the Amplified® Bible (AMP), Copyright © 2015 by The Lockman Foundation. Used by permission. www.Lockman.org.

Scripture quotations marked NKJV are from the New King James Version®. Copyright © 1982 by Thomas Nelson. Used by permission. All rights reserved.

Scripture quotations marked CSB are from the Christian Standard Bible®, Copyright © 2017 by Holman Bible Publishers. Used by permission. Christian Standard Bible® and CSB® are federally registered trademarks of Holman Bible Publishers.

Original artwork by Ruth Chou Simons. Designed by Sarah Alexander.

The prayer at the end of the book is taken from *The Valley of Vision* edited by Arthur Bennett, published by the Banner of Truth Trust, Edinburgh (banneroftruth.org). Used with permission.

Library of Congress Cataloging-in-Publication Data

ISBN 978-1-4002-2998-7 (ITPE)
ISBN 978-1-4002-3657-2 (signed)

Names: Chou Simons, Ruth, author.
Title: When strivings cease : replacing the gospel of self-improvement with the gospel of life-transforming grace / Ruth Chou Simons.
Description: Nashville, Tennessee : Nelson Books, an imprint of Thomas Nelson, [2021] | Includes bibliographical references.
Summary: "Bestselling author, entrepreneur, and speaker Ruth Chou Simons calls women to discover how God's profound gift of grace and favor invites them to rest from chasing approval and earning love, and instead discover the freedom of true belonging and worth that doesn't depend on them"-- Provided by publisher.
Identifiers: LCCN 2021008582 (print) | LCCN 2021008583 (ebook) | ISBN 9781400224999 (hardcover) | ISBN 9781400225002 (epub)
Subjects: LCSH: Christian women--Religious life. | Christian women--Conduct of life. | Success--Religious aspects--Christianity. | Grace (Theology)
Classification: LCC BV4527 .C493 2021 (print) | LCC BV4527 (ebook) | DDC 234--dc23
LC record available at https://lccn.loc.gov/2021008582
LC ebook record available at https://lccn.loc.gov/2021008583

Printed in the United States of America

21 22 23 24 25   LSC   10 9 8 7 6 5 4 3 2 1

*To the GraceLaced community, past and present:
These hard-won truths have shaped every word I write and
every stroke I paint. I can't wait for Grace to amaze you too.*

Buddha's Final Words: Strive unceasingly.
Jesus' Final Words: It is finished.

—TIM KELLER

Contents

Introduction: We're Missing Something (Why We're So Tired.
Why We Strive.)   xi

Part 1: When Striving Isn't Enough

Chapter 1: Bent and Broken: Striving to Please   3

Chapter 2: Unworthy: Striving for Attention   21

Chapter 3: Just Amazing Enough to Not Need Grace:
            Striving to Be Good Enough   33

Chapter 4: The Welcome We Long For: Striving for
            Approval   47

Chapter 5: Pressure to Perform: Striving to Save
            Ourselves Through Perfection   61

Chapter 6: The Lunchroom: Striving to Belong   75

Chapter 7: Honor and Shame: Striving to Outrun
            Shame   87

Chapter 8: The Gift: Striving to Have It All   105

Part 2: When Grace Changes Everything

Chapter 9: Grace Makes New, Not Better   123

CONTENTS

Chapter 10: Grace Fuels Good Works   141
Chapter 11: Grace Cancels Our Debt, For Real   155
Chapter 12: Grace Rewrites Our Stories   171
Chapter 13: Grace Replaces Fear with Freedom   189
Chapter 14: Grace Makes Forgiveness Possible   205
Chapter 15: Grace Is Enough to Hold You Together   219

A Closing Prayer   227
Acknowledgments   229
Notes   233
About the Author   235

Introduction

*We're Missing Something
(Why We're So Tired. Why We Strive.)*

> *All this trying leads up to the vital moment at which you turn to God and say, "You must do this. I can't."*
>
> —C. S. Lewis, *Mere Christianity*

I wish we were sitting down over a cup of coffee, face-to-face, close enough for you to see my chipped nail polish and ungroomed eyebrows (yes, I'm writing you from the middle of 2020's COVID-19 outbreak), or the way I mess with my cuticles when I'm really focused and forming my thoughts—close enough for me to ask you an honest question that's changed everything in my adult life:

If we believe Jesus is all we need, then why do we live our days worn out, fearful, and anxiously striving as if we are lacking and unable to measure up?

- *As if we are lacking—lacking resources, time, achievement, clarity, purpose, energy, confidence . . . or acceptance and welcome from a holy God.*
- *As if we are unable to measure up—as friends, at work, as mothers, as wives, for our parents, with our appearance, in our current season of life . . . as Christ followers.*

I don't know about you, but 2020's unexpected worldwide pandemic revealed some things in my life I conveniently overlook sometimes when everything is "normal." After the initial novelty of staying home, playing board games, and baking with family wore off, the pressure to perform set in. Suddenly, I felt the intense pressure to carpe diem my way through the unfamiliar circumstances, to use this extra time at home to the fullest. I don't know where I thought the expectations were coming from, but I heard them play out in my head: *Learn a language! Create a YouTube channel with helpful content! Set up the most inspiring homeschool environment! Inspire your community and employees! Lead! Set the example! Reorganize your life! Finish home projects!*

I expected maximum productivity and creativity from myself, all while navigating loss, isolation, sadness, stress eating, and perpetual low-grade fear and worry.

Was it just me? Did you notice how easy it was to default to striving our way to assurance and comfort when we felt so much fear and lack of control? Did you notice how shaky we felt about our place in the world when the expectations for social and professional engagement, and productivity, all changed in a moment?

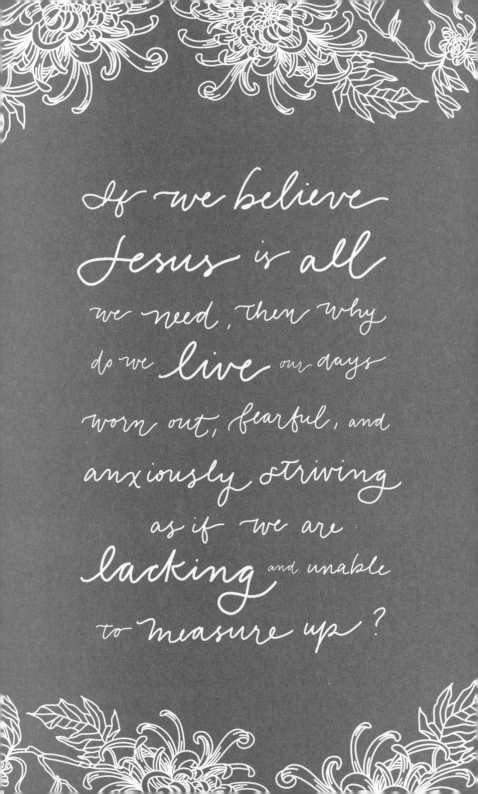

If we believe
Jesus is all
we need, then why
do we live our days
worn out, fearful, and
anxiously striving
as if we are
lacking and unable
to measure up?

The dependencies, routines, and dare I say, idols that were uncovered in my life during this chaotic start to a new decade helped me see how not circumstantial some of my responses were—and that how we seek to fix ourselves reveals what we really believe we need. This plays out even in the books we read and who we listen to for counsel.

An unprecedented number of Christian self-help books populate the current bestsellers lists, and if we were to judge our generation by the covers that line our shelves, we'd gather that, while women have unhindered opportunities for self-made success, empowerment, and freedom to break molds in this generation, we are also more anxious, overwhelmed, and weighed down than ever.

For some of us, these feelings can seem like the soundtrack playing in the background of our daily lives, and sometimes we sing along, asking those anxious questions: What does it take to not miss my purpose? To not miss my potential? To meet expectations? To not waste my life? What does it take to feel like I've done enough? What must I do to *be* enough?

I may not admit it out loud, but so often I'm looking for a formula that ensures my "arrival." I want the fix for the fear of not getting it right. I want to know what I can do to make sure I hit the mark. Is it just me? I don't think so.

The reason our bookshelves look the way they do is that we are all constantly hoping to find our purposes, discover our places in the world, and make peace with what we ourselves, and others, expect of us. These aren't necessarily bad goals—some might even call them good—but why are they leading to so much weariness and uncertainty when the formulas promise the exact opposite?

If someone offers you a prescription for what ails you, but the prescription leaves your condition unchanged, it usually means that something is not quite right about either the prescription or the diagnosis. If what we really need in order to stop feeling so worn out and pressed to perform at a certain standard is a better strategy, then why are the prescriptions not working? We continue reaching for formulas for success, strategies for life direction, or feel-good pep talks that we think must certainly be the fix for our feelings of inadequacy. And I get it. I mean, I'd love to be writing a book of life lessons you could emulate and run with, stories that immediately empower you to *do something*. Because that's what feels right in this culture of hustle. But here's the thing: God has given us a better way, one that, at first, makes you scratch your head and think, *What? How does that make sense?*

And maybe this is why I wish we were on a coffee date. Because then you'd see how seriously I mean it when I say: what actually changed everything for me in this unending search for adequacy, enoughness, whatever you want to call it, was truly understanding God's grace—by which I mean, reclaiming it from its trite usage and looking at it from a biblical point of view—and I almost missed it. It almost seemed too simple, or like there should be more to it, but this is what I've learned takes us from a place of striving to living fully into our spiritual potential as image bearers of a bigger-than-we-think God. I've learned that what I needed was more than the latest prescription; I needed a proper diagnosis and a true solution for my endless striving.

That's the journey I want us to undertake together here. This is not a call to get busy; it's a call to get *discerning*.

Because what we've been busy doing isn't working. We've

This is **not** a call to get **busy**; it's a call to get *discerning*.

gotten out of sync with the foundations of what we believe and why our beliefs about God matter in our everyday lives. My goal is to help you realign with what it really means to trust in the grace of God. And to stop thinking of your relationship with Jesus as something adequate to save you from eternal despair but not enough to secure your identity here and now.

At least that's what my actions say I believe when I trust in Jesus for salvation but trust in myself (think: control and manipulate my circumstances) to navigate life. The weariest, most powerless times of my life have been made so not because there wasn't enough content filled with strategies available for the Christian life, but rather because not enough of that material grounded me in what is actually *life-changing* and not just self-bettering.

Could it be that we are so worn and desperate for ways to better ourselves because we've missed the power, inherent in the grace of God, that eradicates self-improvement altogether?

Is it possible that we keep trying to answer the wrong question—"Am I enough?"—when we're really wanting to know: "Is God enough?"

The answer to the latter will satisfy the first.

In *What's Wrong with the World*, G. K. Chesterton wrote, "The Christian ideal has not been tried and found wanting. It has been found difficult; and left untried."[1] His thought is comforting for me as I think about all the ways I can feel discouraged in my relationship with God and want to give up. Do you feel confused at times with God's job versus your job in the Christian life? It could be because the truth of God's grace, when you really think about it, is outrageous. So we downplay it, sometimes subconsciously, and tend to want to lean back on ourselves. We look at the outlandish claim of the gospel that Jesus accomplishes everything we can't and deem it as less than sufficient for change and transformation in believers. We think we must need to add something more to it. After all, it makes sense for us to also have to pull some weight, right?

We might not say we believe a Jesus-plus-our-efforts idea of the gospel, but when we place our performances on the pedestal of personal progress, we're not relying on the grace of God. We're worshiping the gospel of self-reliance. Self-reliance is something we can control, manipulate, and measure according to our efforts. Grace, on the other hand, is countercultural with its rejection of self-sufficiency and its relinquishing of power. Whether we recognize it or not, our culture is sadly intoxicated with the lure of all that's measurable and based on self-reliance, even for those who claim to represent the gospel of Christ. We say we trust that Jesus is enough, but we spend our lives trying to prove that *we are*, instead.

Finding the gospel old news and antiquated, we end up substituting self-help and formulas for our true means for change—the grace of God.

What wears you out today? Is it the impossible standards? The comparison? The baggage of trying your best and your best not being "good enough?"

I see you, friend—trying to read your Bible and keep a quiet time.

I see you, mama—working to keep up with the latest strategies in parenting so your kids will "turn out right."

I see you, college grad—goal setting and life strategizing, seeking ways to use your gifts and talents for fear of wasting your life.

I see you, sister—feeling behind before you've even started.

I see you, and I am you. I've been in those places more than once, and I'm here to tell you that you don't have to keep living there. The abundant life God has promised his children is so much more than that. Shall we walk there together? This journey is for you; you can start right where you are. And I promise—this will change everything.

PART 1

When Striving Isn't Enough

ONE

❧

Bent and Broken

Striving to Please

*My grace is sufficient for you, for my power is
made perfect in weakness.*

—2 CORINTHIANS 12:9

Your name comes from the word for a willow—bending
easily but not easily broken," my mother said, as she grace-
fully formed the Chinese character for my name, stroke
by stroke, every mark placed in order. I'm an artist. I can't help
but appreciate the pictorial aspect of the Chinese language; each
character tells a story.

With my name, my mother meant for me to know strength.
Hidden within the feminine exterior of the name *Rou*—meaning
soft, gentle, or lovely—was a root of resilience and tenacity.

I'd need exactly those traits as I accompanied my parents from Taiwan to the United States as a child, finding my place in a new land to call home. Learning a new language, new systems, unexpected flavors and textures (hello, Kraft Singles American cheese), and different acceptable norms, values, and standards for beauty (think: tanned skin over pale porcelain) required every bit of adaptability, resilience, and tenacity my mother implied in the lexical origin of my name.

People often marvel that I learned English as quickly as I did but comment on how hard it must have been for my parents and me to adapt to life in the United States. Yes, it's amazing to think of all the ways our little family overcame the obstacles of language, transportation, education, and culture, but the greatest challenge was figuring out what it took to be accepted—and to assimilate.

What is expected of me? How do I fit in? What do other girls wear to a birthday party? Is it better to stand out or to disappear? What kind of lunch box will make people like me? (Hint: in 1980 it was Strawberry Shortcake.) As a first grader, I thought these questions were unique to my personal story of crossing the ocean, learning a new language, and finding friends in a new school, but it turns out these attempts to meet "standard" populate everyone's internal dialogue.

You don't have to be an immigrant to feel well-acquainted with this futile mission. Anyone who has ever moved to a new town, been the new student on campus, started a social media account, found a different friend group, joined a gym, or given her life to Christ understands the question that wells up inside each of us: *What must I do to be enough here?*

I've been leading GraceLaced Co. since its founding in 2013

(some of you may remember when it was solely a blog by the same name in 2007), and because I use online platforms to encourage people through both business and ministry, I'm especially cognizant of how our constant access to curated, well-defined perspectives can contribute to either healthy reorientation of our thoughts or unhealthy condemning self-awareness—the latter always telling us that we're not quite fitting in yet, that we've missed the mark and must endlessly strive to attain it.

This endless striving is what I struggled with in those early days of my youth—and still struggle with today. While being *tenacious* and *not easily broken* can be helpful when adjusting to new environments, the other side of it is sometimes a tendency toward people-pleasing, shape-shifting, and bending oneself to seek another's approval. Resilience can be Malleable and Compliant's tougher older sister. The "You go, girl" armor to our "Am I enough?" Even the dictionary gives *pliable* as a synonym for the word *resilience*. Either quality can be an asset—or a burden. *Bending easily but not easily broken* was simultaneously freeing and oppressing for me. Who doesn't want to know resilience? But somewhere along the way I detoured onto the path toward becoming, instead, someone *pleasing*. Someone others favored.

As a young woman taking cues from my left and my right, from what was spoken and unspoken, applauded and shamed, it sure felt like earning favor was more than a strong suggestion; it was a cultural expectation. While differently expressed, both the Eastern and Western worlds I was caught between considered favor and approval most valuable commodities.

Not much has changed in the world that surrounds us, decades later. Being pleasing—being someone who matters, who belongs, who is favored, liked, popular, fawned over, and admired—has become a global pastime, if not an obsession. As I write, over one hundred million people in the United States alone are scrambling for attention, favor, and popularity on the short-video social media platform known as TikTok. And just yesterday, I read of one popular user losing five hundred thousand followers within a matter of days because of some unfavorable behavior that made for bad PR.

Let's be honest: it's not favor in itself that TikTokers are craving; it's what favor and popularity deliver. Brand partnerships, media attention, book deals, name recognition, a sense of arriving. The ability to please others pays, and we've built our lives around its winnings.

Pleasing others to gain favor or preference has driven millions of dollars in cosmetic surgery, social media campaigns, brand management, and products we reach for every day without even thinking about it. Endlessly chasing approval and affirmation isn't the exception; it's the rule. And the same angst that drives us to secure belonging and acceptance through choosing the right words, posting the right things on social media, doing what's widely accepted, and being the most likable versions of ourselves accompanies us into our lives in Christ. Left unchallenged, this angst leaves us limping along—lacking the joy, hope, peace, assurance, and transformation we expect to experience as believers. A worldly means of favor was never meant to deliver an otherworldly means of grace.

From the conversations I have around my kitchen table to the ones I have with readers around the country, I keep hearing similar stories from women who want to see breakthrough in their lives. They want to break the cycle of worry, fear, weariness, busyness, comparison, or joylessness. They want to feel accepted, known, loved, and enough for what God has called them to do. These are Bible-believing women in church, reading good books, participating in Bible studies, loving their families, serving their communities, and doing hard things. These are women who know what to tell a friend who's questioning her worth and her purpose. These are women who love Jesus. I'm one of these women; I'm guessing you may be too.

I meet so many of you while speaking at Christian events and conferences, and if you only knew—I wrestle with my own enoughness at these events too. I've heard it said that there are authors who speak, and then there are speakers who write books occasionally. I'm the former. Public speaking turns my insides out. For me, it's a combination of lifelong stage fright mixed with the steep learning curve of stage presence after a lifetime of local presence from my kitchen table—and *not* with lights and cameras. I love speaking after I finish the work. I love the opportunity to step out from behind a screen, a beautifully published book, an edited photo, and the packaged artwork that customers receive—and show up as myself, unfiltered, unedited, unpolished: a real middle-aged woman preaching the same truths to herself as she preaches to others. I'm so grateful to be invited and to be entrusted with the hearts of women who come to listen. But the weeks, days, and even moments leading up to my time at the podium before hundreds of thousands are fraught with doubts and convincing narratives:

I'm not funny enough.
I'm not eloquent enough.

I'm not godly enough.
I'm not experienced enough.
I'm not punchy enough.
I'm not animated enough.
I'm not interesting enough.
I'm not knowledgeable enough.
I'm not like [name of any peer I admire] enough.

I promise—these feel ridiculous for me to say out loud (I mean, what is this—middle-aged meets middle school?), and I wouldn't even vulnerably write them out here if I didn't think that you sometimes hear these things whispered in your ear too.

Recently, after having not spoken for some time at an event due to a year of pandemic restrictions, I found myself unnecessarily gripped with fear while preparing for my session at the first major in-person event since COVID-19 cancellations. From a hotel room all alone, I felt the *not-enoughs* crowding out the message I was trying to prepare.

I knew I needed to have a chat with the Lord about what was going on in my heart and mind. I silenced my phone and turned off the music. And confessed aloud to the Lord: "God—you've gotta help me overcome this anxiety if you want me to do this work. You've gotta give me better coping skills, better speaking skills, better stage skills."

And though I heard no audible sound in that hotel room, I did recall his words through the apostle Paul in 2 Corinthians 12:9:

"My grace is sufficient for you, for my power is made perfect in weakness." Therefore I will boast all the more gladly of my weaknesses, so that the power of Christ may rest upon me.

And as I remembered God's provision of grace to Paul, I was sure of his response to me:

It's not about you, child. I get to use you to make much of me if I want to, even if you don't feel the approval or favor you think you need. You don't need to be good enough. You need to be good with me being enough. How else do you think I'm going to deliver a message of grace through you?

I went to the event that night aware of my weaknesses but even more aware of God's faithfulness—before I even got onstage to deliver the closing keynote.

God desires to prove his faithfulness through our surrender in our weaknesses, but so often we choose to resist his help, clinging to our own determination to prove ourselves strong. We'd rather limp along in our striving than surrender in weakness. The reason we limp along and live worn out in our Christian lives is what I hope to uncover in these pages you hold in your hands, and it's what I seek to lead us out of through the means of grace.

In some ways, this journey has to start at the beginning of my story. I've written (and painted) my way through several books, all of which point to foundational truths about God's character, our identity in him, and how we can be rooted in truth through our everyday lives. Each of my previous books has been devotional in nature—meditations and studies that lead us to a deeper walk with the Lord. They've been some of my very favorite projects to date.

But this time, I want to tell you the backstory—the reason I care so much about foundational truths, believe that preaching truth to yourself matters, and advocate for beholding God's greatness in our mundane everyday. Beautiful, inspirational, and even compelling truths can only grow up into maturity when planted in good soil; otherwise, they're just pretty handpicked bouquets—delightful for a time but lacking any sustaining power. The most vibrant florals wilt and fade when not deeply rooted. This book is the hard-won, mended soil I've learned to cultivate in the last two decades of my life.

Good soil—really good soil—isn't just good because of the visible top layer of mulch that keeps it looking fresh and maintained. Good soil is known for its nutrients, substance, and moisture-keeping qualities; it's the stuff beneath the surface that really matters. Good soil seeks to hold on to every bit of thirst-quenching water it receives, and it releases nutrients to the roots established within it. Good soil is the difference between a plant that withers and a plant that grows, and, as Jesus taught, good soil is the difference between truth that transforms and truth that never takes root.

> Hear then the parable of the sower: When anyone hears the word of the kingdom and does not understand it, the evil one comes and snatches away what has been sown in his heart. This is what was sown along the path. As for what was sown on rocky ground, this is the one who hears the word and immediately receives it with joy, yet he has no root in himself, but endures for a while, and when tribulation or persecution arises on account of the word, immediately he falls away. As for what was sown among thorns, this is the one who hears the word, but the cares of the world and the deceitfulness of riches choke the word, and it proves unfruitful. As for what was sown on good soil, this is the one who hears the word and understands

Good soil
is the difference
between truth that
transforms
and truth that
never takes root.

it. He indeed bears fruit and yields, in one case a hundredfold, in another sixty, and in another thirty. (Matt. 13:18–23)

We all live between two worlds. We are planted here on earth while our hope is in heaven. We are given work to do in temporary soil that, we're told, has the potential to spring up into unending fruit. We live in earthly bodies but abide in the eternal. In Christ, we are instantly transferred from dark to light, but we are continually being made new. Present progressive. It's ongoing and actively happening right now. Everything that is ours in Christ is true right now but, at the same time, not fully realized— yet. We are living the now and not yet. And in this in between, we can mistake *not yet* for *not enough* if we're not grounded in what the Bible actually says about God's favor and how we receive it.

We're *not yet* sinless, but his forgiveness is enough to make us clean.

We're *not yet* with him face-to-face, but his presence is enough to sustain us.

We're *not yet* fully transformed, but his glory is enough to declare us worthy.

Instead of deeply rooting ourselves within the substance of God's grace, we keep trying to fit grace into the framework of *our own* soil for success—a framework that feeds on our innate pressure to perform and seeks to sustain a standard that disappoints no one.

That's why we're so tired. That's why we keep hustling. That's why we never feel like we're enough. We're working so hard to bloom, to bend, to please that we've neglected the soil from which we flourish.

I'm convinced we live and act out of what we believe, meaning that what we love most, believe wholeheartedly, and feel most convinced of will dictate the choices we make, the things we prioritize, the fears that consume us, and how we orient our lives.

Getting to the Root of It

I can only assume—in my own life and in yours—that when we run ragged chasing an unobtainable goal for arrival, we're actually being chased down by an Enemy whose lies have been the same from the beginning of time: *God is not trustworthy. You have to be your own hero. You need to know more, be more, do more in order to save yourself . . .* from whatever your worst fear is.

Our culture's answer to "Am I enough?" is always "You are if you believe it!"

We're fed the formula: Soothe your fear of not being enough with achievement. Indulge in the kind of self-love that makes you resilient to anything or anyone that's unloving. Be the best. Replace your sense of lack with control. Keep things neat and tidy. Cover up your exhaustion with religious effort that's too nice to argue with.

The Enemy knows, if we follow this formula, we'll eventually replace the true good news of Jesus Christ—that God's son took on flesh, lived a sinless life, and died on a brutal cross as penalty for our sin, that we might be adopted as sons and daughters of God, sealed by the Holy Spirit, and made alive in Christ, just as he himself resurrected and overcame death—with our own gospel of self-improvement.

I know what you're thinking. *How can self-bettering seem more appealing than Jesus?* Deception wouldn't be doing its job it if looked like a fake. We believe this false gospel because it's almost like the real thing—just a little easier and more convenient to take in. We buy into this formula every single day.

But maybe you've already felt it deep down inside: the strategy for self-improvement is not really working. The race to becoming a more acceptable version of ourselves is simply *not enough*. It has never been enough, and it never will be. I should acknowledge here that many books have been written about this—I *know* I'm not novel in treating this topic of "enoughness," but my goal is not to rehash whether we are enough. Rather, I'm seeking to peel back the layers of *why* we continue in the cycle of thinking enoughness is attainable by our own means. And how all that striving has to do with what we really think about God's grace.

We keep trying to squeeze life out of a means that never matched the end. God gives his freedom and welcome in *his* way. And, truth is, this faulty framework and insufficient understanding of approval leaves us with only one of two options: We either keep striving—bending, maneuvering, adapting—to be what we think is required of us. Or, alternatively, we give up pleasing anyone else—including God—and only seek to please ourselves. You see, friend, if we believe it's up to us to be pleasing and enough, we can only try harder or stop caring altogether. Neither is what God intended for you.

So let's take a moment to be honest with ourselves—a bit of self-diagnosis here at the start. Did you pick up this book because you're always seeking to try harder, or are you on the brink of throwing in the towel with figuring out what God really wants *from* you and *with* you? It's okay if you can't quite answer that just yet, but maybe start with a little assessment. What's your current response when you read about the Christian life in the Bible? Do you feel . . .

- grateful and relieved?
- stressed and guilty?
- tired of trying to figure it out?

You can trace your way back to your core belief by starting with your response. When you believe your only hope is God's grace, you'll respond with gratitude and relief. When you believe it's up to you to perfectly please God, you'll struggle with guilt and fear. And if you believe God is unknowable, unkind, or unfair in what he asks of his creation, you'll stop trying to know him at all. My most anxious, weary, and discouraged times are not simply seasons affected by circumstance; they are seasons shaped by wrong core beliefs about God. What do you find yourself believing in this season?

Even all the way back in the garden of Eden, Eve doubted God—her core belief was that God might be holding out on her. And so her response was reaching out and taking what she believed was lacking in God's plan and provision.

> But the serpent said to the woman, "You will not surely die. For God knows that when you eat of it your eyes will be opened, and you will be like God, knowing good and evil." So when the woman saw that the tree was good for food, and that it was a delight to the eyes, and that the tree was to be desired to make one wise, she took of its fruit and ate, and she also gave some to her husband who was with her, and he ate. (Gen. 3:4–6)

You can't treat the symptom without identifying the cause.

Eve wasn't simply tempted into a momentary lapse in judgment; she acted out of her belief. She believed God's directions and provisions for her good were not enough; she believed she knew better than God.

You can't treat the symptom without identifying the cause.

When I lose my temper and yell at my kids, when I withhold forgiveness in my heart, when I'm careless about what I'm entertained by, I'm acting out of a core belief that I can get where I want to go *my way*.

I want compliance—I use my tone to demand it.

I want justice—and withhold my forgiveness.

I want the comfort distraction brings—and settle for less than what's worthy.

You see, none of those choices are made in the moment; they are formed long before we decide to act on them with our eyes, hands, or lips. What we believe about what God's given and what we think we need determines the choices we make.

We were made to please God alone. He created us out of his good pleasure:

> So God created man in his own image, in the image of God
> he created him; male and female he created them. And God
> blessed them. . . . And God saw everything that he had made,
> and behold, it was very good. (Gen. 1: 27–28, 31)

Sin is our bending away from God and into allyship with our own fears, insecurities, and ineptitude. We fell out of alignment when sin entered the world. As image bearers, our true potential is to reflect—to image—a holy God. That means that we were meant to reflect him. Sin didn't just cause our misalignment; it blocked our ability to truly desire alignment with our Creator, God, as we ought. We've been chasing after alignment with our own ideas and purposes by our own means ever since the fall, bending and trying to fit our form into the ever-changing picture of what it is to be worthy.

And when we bend—straining against what we're created for—we break.

TWO

✦

Unworthy

Striving for Attention

O LORD, you have searched me and known me!
You know when I sit down and when I rise up;
you discern my thoughts from afar.
You search out my path and my lying down
and are acquainted with all my ways.

—PSALM 139:1–3

My childhood years were fraught with all that you'd expect of a kid figuring out how to live between two worlds, eager to tell of my experiences to parents who couldn't relate. After a full day of English speaking and middle school drama, I'd come home and share all the social and emotional details of my American school life. To do so, I'd revert back to Mandarin. I speak Mandarin with my parents, even if I lack vocabulary or true fluency. It's our native tongue, their heart language, and the one thing that's never changed in the past four decades of my life. Though it was challenging to report the day's events in Mandarin, it was worth the effort in order to disclose all the unbelievable details about my middle school life.

On one occasion in seventh grade, the evening download was especially poignant and memorable. I always took forever to finish dinner (not anymore), and with a small home and just the four of us, one of my parents always lingered at the table to work on something parental as I finished my meal. That evening, after a particularly dramatic and socially gruesome day at the prestigious private school I attended on scholarship, I started in on my recounting of all the juicy details after dinner. My father was still at the table, and I was eager to let him into my crazy life. I drew a long breath and told my story—the life-altering truths of my day.

"You won't believe it," I began. "Sarah said mean things about Jenny again. She told everyone that Jenny wanted to be Matt's girlfriend, so Sarah broke up with him and kissed Billy at lunch recess. Jenny was embarrassed and so mad. She spent lunch in the girls' bathroom and locked herself in a stall because she was being dramatic. Then all the popular girls heard about it and found her in the bathroom before fifth period and tried to comfort her. Except Maggie and Lisa's group—they were happy she was sad and went to tell the teacher that everyone was in the bathroom confessing all the things they did last year when they were seventh graders, things they would *never* do now that they've matured. Then, Jenny and Sarah made up and became best friends again. I don't know why, but I don't do anything mean to anyone and none of them ever—"

I stopped, realizing that, while I was fully engrossed in the recounting of my middle-school-girl-drama stories—events that rocked my world and challenged everything I knew about the game of love, boys, and friendship—and was pouring out all the details of my life to my father at the kitchen table, he seemed completely unaware that I was even talking to him.

My father is a quiet man. He shows love through fixing the sink. He's not terribly emotive and rarely weighs in about anything unless asked. But this . . . this was more than quiet. This felt cold.

He didn't look up. He didn't raise an eyebrow, roll his eyes, laugh at the silliness, or even show an ounce of interest. My father wasn't the kind of dad who would invite me over to sit on his lap so he could tell me how precious I was or how these crazy middle school years would soon pass. This wasn't like the scenes I'd seen in the movies or the interactions I'd watch sometimes at friends' houses where American fathers would call their daughters "Daddy's little girl." Honestly, having a cool distance between us was normal. My dad wasn't one to seize the opportunity to make sure I felt seen, known, loved, or wanted. He wasn't particularly eager to be a safe place for me.

On this evening, though, I had feelings I wanted him to acknowledge. I had expectations, and they weren't being met. It felt difficult to share all the details of my life, and I wanted a response. I was ready to call him out for his lack of engagement this time. (How could he not care about these events of my day?!)

"Why don't you ever care or respond when I talk to you?"

I demanded, feeling justified in my frustration after disclosing such personal, intimate details about my preteen life.

My father's succinct response, instead, broke through that momentary silence without a hint of emotion, explanation, or empathy. He shut me down with six simple words: "*Ni hai mei you xi wan.*"

Translation: "You have not finished the dishes."

I remember being speechless (which, turns out, is very rare for me) and instantly went silent. I grabbed the dish soap, squirted some on the scrub brush, and filled up the sink with water. I closed my mouth and finished the dishes.

My parents were incredibly industrious people, working multiple jobs to provide for my brother and me. They came to true saving faith as I was entering high school, the same point at which I surrendered my life to Christ. In some ways, my parents and I were infants in our faith together. This perspective helps me process some of those formative years of life. Now that I'm in my forties, I have a knowing appreciation for what it took to simultaneously make a living, learn new norms, raise children who assimilated quickly (too quickly), and to do so all while learning when to hold on tighter and when to let go in the war of worlds.

But those six words shaped much of my view of God for a very long time.

You have not finished the dishes.

What implications did I internalize from those six words?

- What I do is more important than who I am.
- I'm not worthy of his time if I'm not doing a good job.
- The details of my life aren't interesting to my father unless they have to do with what I'm getting done.

- You have to earn your right to be paid attention to.
- I can't ask for anything if I haven't held up my end of the deal.
- I shouldn't expect empathy if I'm not perfectly empathetic.
- I get what I deserve, so I should become deserving.

And that internal dialogue became the framework for how I perceived the Lord as my heavenly Father. I internally imagined him saying:

- *You haven't read your Bible—don't come to me until you do.*
- *You haven't made the right choices—don't cry for help now that you're in trouble.*
- *You haven't acted very Christlike—clean yourself up before you draw near.*

No one told me to draw those conclusions; they just came naturally. We don't have to try very hard to have an inadequate, incomplete view of God. Or to project the realities of our earthly fathers onto our expectations of our heavenly Father. We're hardwired to fill in all the gaps of our unknowns with trust in no one else but ourselves.

That's what idolatry is. It's aligning our hearts' allegiance and love to anything less than the true recipient of our worship: God himself.

I'll be honest—for me, that idol can easily be my own control and what I think it takes to maintain it. If the serpent found a willing ally in Eve to doubt God's promises and sovereign care, all while both Adam and Eve had unhindered fellowship with

God, how much more are we susceptible to believing wrongly about who God is when we have imperfect fatherhood modeled for us by earthly, human dads?

Because we naturally form patterns of thought in our minds based on our feelings, we must be intentional about replacing our faulty ideas of God with what is actually true about who he is and what he desires from us. Otherwise, we will operate out of self-pity, self-condemnation, our sense of guilt, and the cultural cues that define our worthiness.

Imagine all that I forfeited with an inaccurate picture of God and his availability to me: assurance, peace, comfort, strength, joy, freedom; so much missed simply because I believed wrongly about what I needed in order to come, and *keep coming*, to God.

Let me be honest here about a perennial struggle I have with coming to God, again and again. Every year Troy, my husband, and Caleb, my oldest son, complete a one-year-through-the-Bible reading plan through their ESV app. They're both wired to love routine and slow mornings. They both read voraciously and consistently, undistracted by the demands of social media. Every year I try to do the same, but I'm just the opposite. I'm not a morning person, not terribly good at routine, and easily distracted by more pressing and seemingly productive tasks that give me the results I think I need and get me ahead (ahem—thus the topic of this book, friend). Most of the time, during a Bible reading plan, I get stuck somewhere in Leviticus or the Minor Prophets and fall behind with the schedule. While I know in my head that the schedule is not what saves me, I'm still tempted to pull away and give up when I've "failed" to stay on track.

An inaccurate view of God—that he's unavailable until we do our part—will cause us to think that something replenishing, like

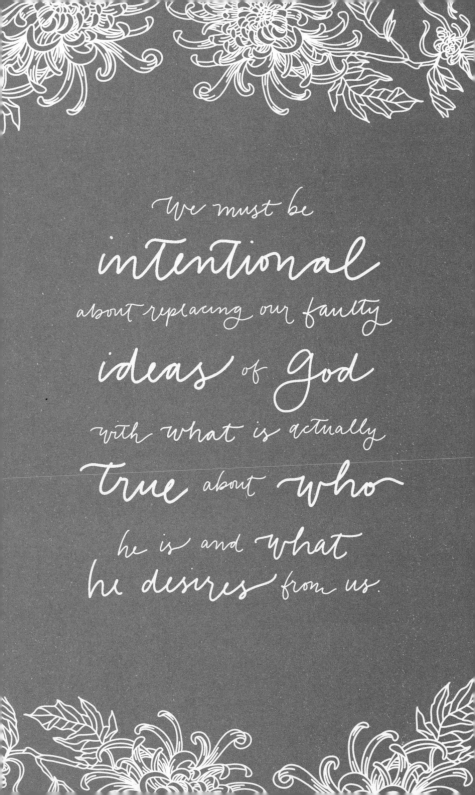

We must be *intentional* about replacing our faulty *ideas* of *God* with what is actually *true* about *who* he is and *what* *he desires* from us.

reading our Bibles, is about us and our accomplishment and not about God and his invitation. We stay away and forfeit the welcome we have in Christ when our ability to draw near is informed by a faulty view of God.

What faulty views of God do you have? Do your beliefs about what kind of Father he is line up with the Bible? Let's take a moment to look at what Scripture tells us. I don't want to just tell you about him; I don't want you to just take my word for it. I need you to know how welcomed you are through Christ—but take his word on it, instead.

- *He is patient with us.* "The Lord, the Lord, a God merciful and gracious, slow to anger, and abounding in steadfast love and faithfulness" (Ex. 34:6).
- *He calls us sons and daughters.* "He predestined us for adoption to himself as sons through Jesus Christ, according to the purpose of his will" (Eph. 1:5).
- *He is a tender father we needn't fear.* "You did not receive the spirit of slavery to fall back into fear, but you have received the Spirit of adoption as sons, by whom we cry, 'Abba! Father!'" (Rom. 8:15).
- *He knows our frailty yet has compassion on us.* "As a father has compassion on his children, so the Lord has compassion on those who fear him. For he knows our frame; he remembers that we are dust" (Ps. 103:13–14).
- *He knows everything about us (and made us lovingly).* "O Lord, you have searched me and known me! You know when I sit down and when I rise up; you discern my thoughts from afar. You search out my path and my lying down and are acquainted with all my ways. . . . For you

formed my inward parts; you knitted me together in my mother's womb" (Ps. 139:1–3, 13).

- *He invites us in and makes us family.* "So then you are no longer strangers and aliens, but you are fellow citizens with the saints and members of the household of God" (Eph. 2:19).
- *He makes us able to draw near with confidence.* "Let us then approach God's throne of grace with confidence, so that we may receive mercy and find grace to help us in our time of need" (Heb. 4:16 NIV).
- *He listens to the detail and fears and burdens we bear, and he responds.* "You heard my plea: Do not ignore my cry for relief. You came near whenever I called you; you said, 'Do not be afraid.' You championed my cause, Lord; you redeemed my life" (Lam. 3:56–58 CSB). (If you read all of Lamentations 3 you find a beautiful example of pouring one's heart out to the Lord—in detail.)

You're the only one who knows the well-worn path in your pattern of thought when it comes to God, our heavenly Father. You may say with your lips, "He is faithful. He is good." But do your actions reveal a different truth?

When we believe an earthly father is available, knowable, inviting, and good, we go running to him. We don't hesitate to pursue a father who welcomes us with open arms, who looks up from his work and really listens, who shows concern when we cry, who holds us when we ache, who's patient with our petty complaints and silly stories. In the same way, we go running to God when we believe him to be that kind of Father. But we shy away and guard ourselves more when an earthly father doesn't

What we believe about our Father determines how we come to him — or if we come at all.

pursue us or seems silent. When he is bad at listening or isn't available. We hide. We stay away. We pretend.

What we believe about our Father determines how we come to him—or if we come at all.

What's keeping you from drawing near to your Father? Are you coming to him hindered? Fearful? Feeling unworthy? Are you coming defensively? Lacking ears to hear? Whatever it is, the first step in this journey is tracing your way backward from your present view of God. Where does it lead you?

Does it lead you back to the Word of God and what Scripture says about him?

Does it lead you back to your own sense of guilt, shame, or unworthiness?

Does it lead you back to an idea that's been modeled imperfectly by imperfect family members?

Everything God says about himself in the Word of God and every way he's revealed himself to creation and to his children has always been to declare:

I am faithful, in spite of your faithlessness.

So if you find yourself constantly trying to work toward being deemed worthy of God's attention, thinking you have to be enough before you can be fully welcomed, assuming his love and faithfulness is only in place if your actions are perfect, take a step back. Find your way to the firm foundation of who the Bible says he is. And remember:

You are welcome, even when you haven't been consistently in the Word.

You are invited, even when your faith is lacking.

You are loved, even if you're ashamed of your track record.

THREE

Just Amazing Enough to Not Need Grace

Striving to Be Good Enough

Amazing grace,
how sweet the sound
that saved a wretch like me.
I once was lost but now am found,
was blind but now I see.

—JOHN NEWTON, "AMAZING GRACE"

f I am honest, I'd say I spent much of my early Christian life singing "Amazing Grace" while living like the words were actually "God, let me be so amazing that I won't need grace."

As I unpacked a bit already, despite access to good churches, a Christian college, and a seemingly good foundation in the Christian faith, I eventually found myself spiraling in an effort to prove myself, secure myself, and flailing in my faith when I couldn't measure up. Hiding the shame of walking away from the privilege afforded me as a dual enrollment high school student taking undergrad classes at UC Berkeley, and the disappointment of forfeiting some of the most promising scholarships I could receive at other schools (including a full ride at Westmont College), I moved back home my second year of college and returned to the state school in my hometown, in New Mexico. In that same season I sabotaged a multiyear relationship with a good and kind young man I'd thought I would marry.

I was deeply heartbroken and ashamed. I couldn't forgive myself but learned to distract my pain. My hidden shame and secret turmoil had been stacking against me despite the respectable, responsible, even enviable exterior I'd managed to maintain. No one knew how confused I felt. Some of us are pros at making our mistakes look intentional, neatly wrapped up, and quickly forgotten in the light of our achievements. Some of us can deflect pain with a convincingly perfect performance. That was me.

Running from that which was difficult, from my disappointment in myself, had so become my modus operandi that my path of least resistance led me right back to my hometown, unable to figure out what I really wanted or where I was going. In God's kindness and sovereignty, my need for distraction led me to join a collegiate ministry—the Baptist Student Union at the University of New Mexico (now called Christian Challenge). I started going about the same time that the collegiate minister in that season, Dale, began teaching weekly through the Sermon on the Mount in Matthew 5. As can be the case for many raised in the church, though, all the stories were familiar. And, if I was honest, they felt irrelevant to what I was going through and the decisions I was facing.

The gospel can feel like old news if we believe it merely good for salvation and miss its potency for true life. That's where I was when I walked into the Baptist Student Union. The gospel felt stale to me—the stuff of Vacation Bible School—and more like a membership card than an active lifeline. I didn't see how the gospel could have any bearing on my life right then. To me, it was simply a line in the sand for those who chose heaven over hell.

Dale, who later became a dear friend and mentor to both Troy and me, clearly and deliberately called our attention to Jesus' teaching. As simple as the message was, I heard it then for the astounding truth that it was with clarity—perhaps for the first time. This is the passage Dale read aloud:

> You have heard that it was said to those of old, "You shall not murder; and whoever murders will be liable to judgment." But I say to you that everyone who is angry with his brother will be liable to judgement; whoever insults his brother will be liable to the council; and whoever says, "You fool!" will be liable to the hell of fire. . . .
>
> You have heard that it was said, "You shall not commit adultery." But I say to you that everyone who looks at a woman with lustful intent has already committed adultery with her in his heart. (Matt. 5: 21–22, 27–28)

I remember feeling called out, though I had clearly never thought of myself as being on par with a murderer or adulterer.

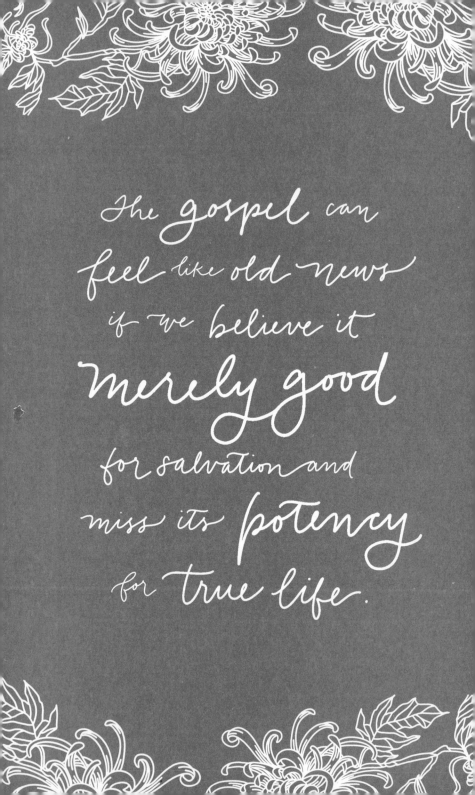

The gospel can feel like old news if we believe it merely good for salvation and miss its potency for true life.

But I knew all my regrettable mistakes. I knew how I'd used my words to cut and tear down. I knew the ways I'd dishonored the Lord with the opposite sex. Hearing these words as they were read to an entire room full of college students, I felt exposed. My secret sins might as well have been on display, scrolling across a jumbotron: *Hey, you, little miss perfect Chinese girl in the back. You're not fooling anyone. You're a failure. Your best isn't good enough. You're not good enough. You'll never be good enough.*

And then I heard these words explaining what Jesus said, and they changed everything: "Unless your righteousness exceeds that of the scribes and Pharisees, you will never enter the kingdom of heaven" (v. 20).

Dale continued, "God set the bar high. Man tried to reach it through self-righteousness, so God set it higher—higher than we can jump."

In that moment it finally clicked for me. Even though I had understood and acknowledged that Jesus died to pay the penalty for my sin and canceled the debt that I owed him, the gospel finally made sense in a complete way.

I can never be good enough, jump high enough, perform well enough to *not need grace.*

I can't help but say it again in case you let it roll over you the first time. This is important.

You and I can never be good enough, jump high enough, perform well enough to not need grace.

If that discourages you or causes you to slump your shoulders in frustration, you've missed the good news. I wonder, Christ follower, would we be so exhausted if we actually grasped how good the good news really is? If Jesus breaks us free of the chains that bound us to our hamster wheel of striving and measuring up, then why would we run back to those chains, dragging around a weight of expectation and condemnation day by day?

It was true in my life and it may be for you, as well: we can't know true freedom if we expect grace to make us merely better, rather than completely new. Better seeks to measure up; completely new requires a miracle.

We sell ourselves short when we receive the gift of God's forgiveness and his grace as a self-betterment strategy—as self-help. He wants nothing less than all of you and all of me. Not just our tough seasons, our unexpected times of trial, our desperate prayers when we have nowhere else to turn, or our pleading for strength to meet a goal. He might meet us there to start, but he's in the business of total transformation, not a plan for improvement or one TV makeover episode.

Growing up, I was no stranger to the pursuit of self-betterment, of being *amazing*. In my mind, it looked like straight As, graduating with honors, winning piano competitions, staying home to study, respecting my elders, signing up for the hardest classes, and having letters after your name. It looked like titles, resumes, and getting ahead by never rocking the boat. It's okay if you don't relate to this, but we'll be better friends if you know this about me:

I once thought anything less than getting into Stanford or MIT was wasting your life.

I declared a biochem major just because it seemed like the right thing to do for someone taking a class in engineering calculus at UC Berkeley while finishing high school.

After fifteen years of piano lessons, I wanted to learn jazz, but instead I signed up for the most difficult piece I could find by Franz Lizst just to top some unspecified standard in my mind.

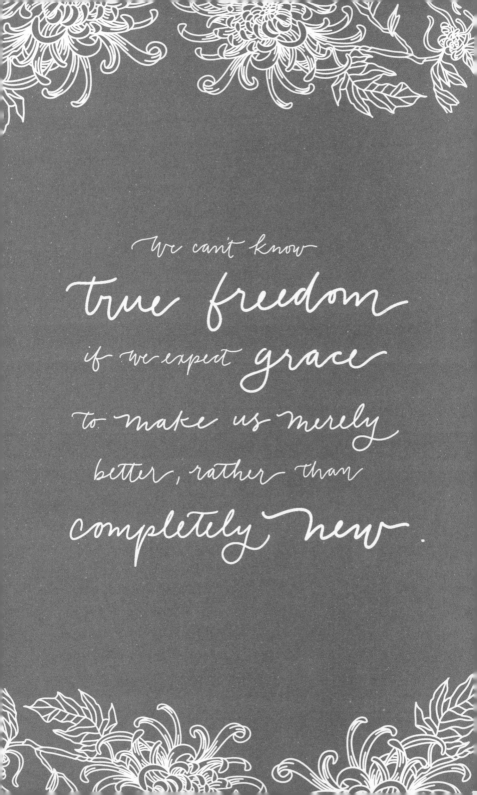

We can't know true freedom if we expect grace to make us merely better, rather than completely new.

At seventeen, I wore myself out with credential collecting. Academically, college-advisors prescribed all the best things to have on your college application, and I was determined to check each off my list and then some. At home, the badges of honor were invisible, only understood through affirmation or disapproval, warmth or aloofness, pride or utter disappointment. Badges and credentials aren't always visible, but they're so often felt.

The problem with chasing achievement is that it leaves you with only two options: be enslaved to ever-increasing demands to achieve (because you actually never "arrive") or give up in defeat. My sophomore year of college, when I saw myself reflected in the Sermon on the Mount, I finally began to see that my giving up after a string of disappointments was not just a dreaded dissolution of expecting myself to be amazing. It was really the beginning to finding just how amazing Jesus is.

Maybe you're familiar with the apostle Paul (yep, "The Apostle Formerly Known as Saul"). I can't think of a better example of someone who had "amazing" as part of his resume and credentials. Before God confronted him and redeemed his life on the road to Damascus (see Acts 9—we'll look at it in the next chapter), he was actively persecuting believers as a most upstanding, overachieving, rule-following Pharisee.

> Though I myself have reason for confidence in the flesh also. If anyone else thinks he has reason for confidence in the flesh, I have more: circumcised on the eighth day, of the people of Israel, of the tribe of Benjamin, a Hebrew of Hebrews; as to the law, a Pharisee; as to zeal, a persecutor of the church; as to righteousness under the law, blameless. (Phil. 3:4–6)

But Paul, surrendered to Jesus Christ, described his transformation thus:

> But whatever gain I had, I counted as loss for the sake of Christ. Indeed, I count everything as loss because of the surpassing worth of knowing Christ Jesus my Lord. For his sake I have suffered the loss of all things and count them as rubbish, in order that I may gain Christ and be found in him, not having a righteousness of my own that comes from the law, but that which comes through faith in Christ, the righteousness from God that depends on faith—that I may know him and the power of his resurrection, and may share his sufferings, becoming like him in his death, that by any means possible I may attain the resurrection from the dead. (vv. 7–11)

Notice his choice of words: *whatever, everything, all things, not . . . my own.*

These are 180 words—descriptions of a total turning, a complete transformation, 180 degrees from where he was headed. Paul didn't become a better version of himself or a godlier Jew; Paul became completely God's.

How would you describe the grace of God in your life? Is it the boost you need when you're struggling? The empowerment that helps you do better? Is it *sometimes* your hope, *some* of the change in your life, and *a part* of what makes you get up in the morning?

God didn't give us the standard of righteousness in Matthew 5 (or through any other law of God, more on that later) so that we could meet it in ourselves, but that we might recognize that Jesus met all of it on our behalf. This is grace.

If your idea of grace has been that it's a crutch for the weak, a mantra for the doing-my-best crowd, or the nice thing you say to yourself until you make yourself better, you're missing out.

If you've been feeding on the idea of grace as a pass, a group hug, or a jolly Santa-like God the Father telling you, "Hey, child. No big deal. Your complaining, your worrying, your unhappiness—no worries. You're fine just the way you are," you're missing out.

Friend, I was missing out.

Simply put, God demonstrated through the law that we could never be enough so his love, provision, goodness, holiness, power, and faithfulness would be seen for what it truly is: our only way to being enough to stand before a holy God.

And here's where I fear we stop in our Christian lives, flip the page spiritually, and start looking for our personal game plans—now that we're "okay" before God. We thank him for rescuing us but so often miss the part where he wants *relationship* with us.

God doesn't stop there at making us fit to stand before his presence.

He goes the distance, sheltering us with his love, and marks us favored for his purpose.

Not just fit but favored.

Not just enough to not receive rejection but more than enough to be welcomed in.

In the kingdom, the opposite of amazing isn't disappointing; it's appointed.

Here's what I mean: When we wrongly think that the gospel simply makes us better, we will endlessly strive in our own strength. But when we receive the grace of God as our only credential—the one thing that gives us a place and purpose in

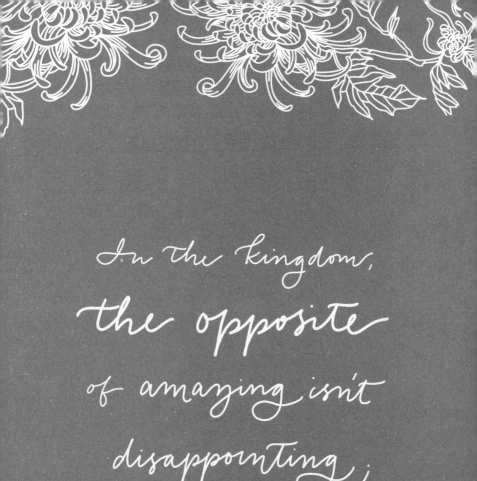

In the kingdom,
the opposite
of amazing isn't
disappointing ;
it's appointed.

the kingdom of God—we live as those appointed, given the power and authority of the Father for all that he's given us to do.

> *Amazing grace, how sweet the sound,*
> *that saved a wretch like me.*
> *I once was lost, self-reliant, fearful, and*
> *anxiously trying to make my life matter,*
> *but now I'm found and favored, appointed*
> *and not a disappointment.*
> *I was blind, but now I see.*

Lord, help us to see.

FOUR

The Welcome
We Long For

Striving for Approval

*Am I now trying to win the approval of human
beings, or of God? Or am I trying to please
people? If I were still trying to please people, I
would not be a servant of Christ.*
—GALATIANS 1:10 NIV

Mom and Dad, I'm going to be an artist."

The last words any Asian parent expects to hear out of their
kids' mouths.

All these years later, I still clearly remember the day I came home and announced I was planning to graduate in three years—and also to change my major to fine arts. My parents were somewhat unconventional in the Chinese community—one a Chinese language arts teacher and writer, and one a business owner in Taiwan turned electronic technician in America—neither terribly conformist, neither driven solely by money or success. Neither of them had, at the time, multiple letters after their names that signified the number of zeroes on their paychecks, and they didn't choose to verbally pressure me into academic achievement as many of my Asian peers felt. The Chinese community we were a part of embodied the expectations enough that I put pressure on myself with no additional parental help at all. If you've befriended an Asian or have ever hung out for any amount of time with an Asian family, you've probably experienced some version of this cultural norm to achieve. Though the arts run deep in Asian cultures, the study of art (and other forms of creative arts) isn't one of those acceptable career trajectories.

I recently heard Jon Yao, a successful young chef of Taiwanese descent and owner of Kato, the famed Michelin-starred restaurant in a Los Angeles strip mall, say in a short documentary, "Cooking isn't a glorified career in East-Asian cultures, so I just wanna not disappoint my entire family. I was on a different career trajectory when I was in college, and I just suddenly dropped everything and started cooking. So I don't want my parents to feel like they wasted their efforts on me."[1] I get you, Jon. "I grew up in an East-Asian household. Your parents are always just like, 'If you're gonna play, you might as well win.'"[2] Again, yes, Jon. That. Exactly that.

Even if my parents were not as hardcore about success,

winning, and career choices as their peers, I knew my switching from biochemistry to fine arts would give them pause.

My dad makes a sound just under his breath when he's thinking, as if holding back the floodgates of his thoughts. Most of my life, I've heard only the restraint and rarely the words he's forming. As I mustered up the courage to speak those life-changing words, I imagined him assessing our American dream ledger as he murmured:

Checklist for us:

- ☑ Move to America.
- ☑ Learn a new language.
- ☑ Work multiple jobs.
- ☑ Provide opportunities for our kids.

Checklist for the kids:

- ☑ Get into good schools.
- ☑ Declare excellent majors.
- ☐ Have good lives.
- ☐ Be successful enough to take care of us when we're old

To be fair, my parents had never suggested or expected that I become a rocket scientist or neurosurgeon. But I had eyes that could see what approval looked like. I had ears that could hear tone and overhear concerns. I knew and felt the social currency all around me—the currency of respect and admiration. And admiration earned favor, and favor brought welcome.

So, I could do the math: gather up enough qualifications to gain respect and admiration, and you'll ultimately receive the welcome you long for. In one decision to change my course of study, I felt as though I were discarding any opportunity for welcome, favor, or admiration. Was I sure I wanted to do this? Was I crazy to run in the exact opposite direction of the laid-out path to approval?

I'd love to say this new plan for my life was well thought out. That I had prayed and fasted or sought wise counsel. (I didn't.) Or that I had already found freedom in my new identity in Christ. (I hadn't.) It'd make for a much better illustration if that were the case. But truth is, it was a decision made out of inner mutiny and fear of failure. After years and years of striving, I simply wore out. I had a full-on case of striving fatigue, and art felt like the remedy. I didn't choose art because I believed I would succeed; I chose art so no one would expect me to. Choosing the path of least resistance—a path so disappointing that I couldn't mess it up—became my perceived way out of the spiral of striving.

Have you known this kind of weary anxiousness, friend? Think about the last time you were stressed over a decision. Trace the path of indecisiveness or anxiety over that decision back to its origin and see if you find a fear of not having welcome, favor, or admiration. Look closely to see if perhaps fear of disappointing others was at the root. I know how often this is true for me.

But isn't acceptance what *we all* long for? What we are constantly spinning and hustling and yearning for? We want welcome. We need welcome. We want an invitation to come near, to stay awhile, and to belong. That's what welcome is. Welcome from friends, welcome from family members, welcome at church, welcome in society, welcome in our jobs, a welcome from our God. Our desire for welcome drives much of our fear—and motivation.

It's always been about welcome for me. Not the kind that

comes with a cozy blanket but the welcome that says, "You are wanted, you are seen, you are known, and you belong." Maybe the same is true for you.

Disappointment

In my last year of college, I landed a job at the well-respected nuclear research and development headquarters in the Southwest, Sandia National Laboratories. For competitive college students with professional aspirations, landing a part-time opportunity there was a golden ticket, coveted in a sea of available openings waiting tables and delivering pizza. I had the grades and a family friend who pulled some strings. I was grateful, even if the job was to record material safety data sheets (riveting, I know).

But somewhere in the middle of what should have been an ideal set of circumstances for an academic mover and shaker, I hit a wall. My then beau, now husband, Troy, who'd also started a job in the same department (helped by his connection to a cute overachieving Chinese gal), had broken up with me, and it felt like a thousand daggers through the heart to see him every day at work. (I'm not proud of the drama—just telling it like it is.) I met with my supervisor to let her know I planned to leave my job.

She looked across the table at me, with both concern and disappointment, and said, "Do you want to turn out like your parents?"

I knew what she meant—she didn't want me to struggle financially, to lack position or title, to juggle multiple jobs in order to make ends meet, to work to earn respect in a culture whose awards were more merit-based than heart-based.

She meant well, I truly believe. She only counseled me based on her worldview concerning worth, value, and acceptance. She was trying to save me from a life of disappointment.

What she couldn't see was that I already felt like a disappointment. A fraud. A joke. A could-have-been.

Thrown-away scholarships, ruined romantic relationships, a career in science forfeited for an imaginary career in art, a mom with emotional baggage I couldn't help carry, a dad who showed little interest in me, years of Sunday school answers that didn't add up to a life of freedom—yes, I felt disappointing. Though I didn't plan on developing a career in the sciences, acquiring a job at the Labs was merit-affirming, and that was a difficult addiction to break. Quitting was just another disappointment in a long line of failures I'd been racking up on my personal scoreboard.

And sometimes when you're disappointed in where you are in a specific season, you start wondering about what influences have affected where you've been. Wrapped up in all my sense of personal lack was an overarching distrust in my upbringing, my culture, my family, my foundations. The disappointment I felt toward myself was knotted and bound up in my disappointment in others—in the way others made me feel. It's so easy to blame someone else for the ways you can't own your own life.

How come I can't do anything right? Will I ever arrive? Does Jesus actually love me "just as I am" if no one else seems to? Why do I feel so much pressure?

My pride didn't want to lay down the idol of perfection—in myself or in others. It wanted to keep striving for it. I know people-pleasing doesn't seem like a pride issue, but if we're honest, it really is. I want to believe I can be exactly who everyone wants me to be if I try hard enough. But my pride also wants to believe that *others*, then, should be exactly who I want *them* to be. If I'm showing up to please them, they should be showing up to please me. Anything less than meeting my standards is disappointing. Disappointment—the kind where our expectations are unmet—so often seeps out of the kind of pride that sneaks up on you.

We know we're lacking in our lives. So we try to make ourselves complete and *not* lacking. Our efforts make us prideful, even though we still question if we've done enough. Because we don't believe we're hopeless enough or that God is merciful enough, we become driven by merit rather than grace. But we end up feeling disappointed all the time because our standards are defined not by God's ability but our own. And we're trying to hold others up to the same standards.

If disappointment in others reveals pride, disappointment in yourself reveals shame (more on this to come). Neither finds its way to hope unless what's wrong is made right.

Some of us know both forms of disappointment like lifelong companions. When one is present, the other is sure to be close at hand. The same person annoyed with another's boasting often hides behind her own desperation to be seen. As a mom, I so often find that the person requiring faultless decision-making in my children (me) is the same person who wrestles with shame from my own perceived failings to choose wisely. It's no wonder, then, that confessing our need for the gospel before our kids impacts the way they receive the expectations we imperfectly place on them.

I didn't (and still don't) need to be disappointed in my parents or my past. I needed to know that expectations placed on me and expectations I placed on others were dead ends in themselves. I

Disappointment in others reveals *pride*; disappointment in yourself reveals **shame**.

needed someone to tell me that avoiding disappointment could never give me what I really wanted: true welcome.

Why do we wrestle so much with all this? I think it has something to do with sin puffing us up so that we are more obsessed with increasing our own capabilities than increasing our awe and wonder in the character of God. I think it has to do with not knowing who he really is enough to be more overwhelmed by him than we are by our need to prove our own worth.

Here's the thing: we picture self-righteousness as Pharisees in long robes, holy rule followers, folks dressed in their Sunday best heading into extravagant church buildings. We rarely picture hardworking, considerate, golden rule–following, upstanding members of society; we rarely picture ourselves. But my hope as you read these words is that you'll feel the sting, as I have, that self-righteousness is sometimes subtle and often deceptive. Our very tendency to think ourselves *not as bad as her* is self-righteousness.

But, friend, if it stings, know that this means you're really alive to what the truth should do. You're not in a numbed stupor. We can't receive relief we don't think we need. Paul the Apostle told it like it is when he said, "None is righteous, no, not one; no one understands; no one seeks for God. All have turned aside; together they have become worthless; no one does good, not even one" (Rom. 3:10–12).

I chafe a bit when I read these verses. I want to defend myself, saying, "You don't know me—I'm one of the good guys! I have good motives. I love Jesus!"

Paul the Apostle, here in Romans, was doing the opposite of tickling our ears or boosting our self-esteem; he was pulling back the layers of our pride, self-improvement, and qualifications and holding up the blindingly bright standard of God's holiness.

Of all people, Paul knew what that felt like.

Back when he was Saul, he was the guy his peers cheered, admired, and held up as the example of worthiness. He had hustle, drive, and a list of achievements that rivaled any Jew.

But God stopped him in his tracks, literally.

Meanwhile, Saul was still breathing out murderous threats against the Lord's disciples. He went to the high priest and asked him for letters to the synagogues in Damascus, so that if he found any there who belonged to the Way, whether men or women, he might take them as prisoners to Jerusalem. As he neared Damascus on his journey, suddenly a light from heaven flashed around him. He fell to the ground and heard a voice say to him, "Saul, Saul, why do you persecute me?"

"Who are you, Lord?" Saul asked.

"I am Jesus, whom you are persecuting," he replied. "Now get up and go into the city, and you will be told what you must do."

The men traveling with Saul stood there speechless; they heard the sound but did not see anyone. Saul got up from the ground, but when he opened his eyes he could see nothing. So they led him by the hand into Damascus. For three days he was blind, and did not eat or drink anything. (Acts 9:1–9 NIV)

God was after his heart. He was after Saul's surrender to the true God, not Saul's self-righteous fervor to achieve within a system of religiosity. Saul's impressive credentials, self-discipline, and follow-through (I mean, did you catch how he was seeking brownie points and going above and beyond to convict anyone not adhering to the law?) didn't win him favor with the Lord. God wanted to change everything about Saul, to shape his life as Paul instead.

It wasn't enough just to improve or amend Saul's worldview; God shut it down completely, causing him to be utterly dependent (temporarily without sight!) and humbled to the core.

God wants our true worship, not our perfect performance. And what should stop us in our tracks when we read this account of Paul's conversion is that God pursued him and transformed his life *while* he was still self-righteous, prideful, hateful, wrong. While he was missing the mark and lacking. While he was disappointed in everyone else. While he was disappointing God himself.

God rescued Paul at the height of his arrogance and achievement. All Paul had to do was fall and bow down. All he had to do was surrender and obey.

Romans 3:23 reminds us, "All have sinned and fall short of the glory of God." Against the glory of God, we, in our natural unredeemed state, are all disappointments. We've all missed the mark. Believing and thinking anything different keeps us in an endless cycle of thinking ourselves capable of saving ourselves.

The holiness of God found us lacking.

The mercy of God sent Jesus to bear the punishment we deserve.

The righteousness of God declared us forgiven.

The goodness of God reshapes us into his likeness.

The love of God overcomes evil so that we might share in all that is Christ's.

It's hard to feel disappointment when you think of all God

God wants
our
true
worship,
not our perfect
performance.

has accomplished for your good and your redemption. When God is great, our met expectations can't be. Striving to avoid disappointment becomes an empty sales pitch. Turns out, all our efforts to skirt the feelings of disappointment keep us from the very surrender we were meant to know. We were meant to experience the reality and disappointment of never being enough in our own merits and abilities.

It's really good news, friend. In our own strength, standing in our own track records, we don't measure up. You don't. I don't. Your pastor doesn't. Your spouse can't. The parent that failed won't. Your kids never will.

You and I are freed from disappointment in others and disappointment in ourselves, not because we can let it go but because God stops us in the middle of our striving and comes after us. *He doesn't let us go*—let us go on in our merit building, approval chasing, people pleasing, or measuring up. He meets us right where pride and shame have left us stuck and disappointed—and sets out the welcome mat of grace for me and for you. We need only to leave where we've been and step in.

FIVE

Pressure to Perform

Striving to Save Ourselves

Through Perfection

> *I was like a man in a bog. The more he struggles,*
> *the more he sinks. Or like a prisoner upon the*
> *treadmill, who rises no higher, but only wearies*
> *himself by his climbing. No good can result from*
> *efforts made apart from faith in Jesus.*
> —CHARLES HADDON SPURGEON

My kids don't believe me when I tell them I used to think I was going to be a concert pianist. I'm pretty sure it's a common assumption among 99.9 percent of all Asian kids who begin studying piano at age three and graduate to Liszt's Études and Chopin's Impromptus as young teens. Honestly: concert pianist and neurosurgeon—the combo isn't unheard of in Chinese circles. I practiced hours a day, training my fingers to submit to the awkward order of notes played on keys that didn't sound remotely pretty to listen to until a good four months into practicing. I wish I could tell you that the ultimate goal for all that practice then was to truly enjoy music. It wasn't. It was to win—at talent shows, piano competitions—and to not lose. It was to excel at something I was expected to do.

The only problem was that I had a pretty overwhelming relationship with stage fright (remember? I told you it was a lifelong issue). I'd be sick to my stomach—anxious over the possibility of tripping on stage, looking foolish, playing the wrong notes, or forgetting my music altogether.

The last fear happened one time, and I'll never forget it. A year of practice and pressure culminated at one performance before a panel of judges. And I froze halfway through. Completely forgot the notes that came next. My face turned hot and bright red as I placed my hands in my lap, stood up, and walked out of the room, ashamed. All my preparation hadn't ensured the result I was after. My execution was flawed, but was it because I hadn't practiced enough? Trained hard enough? Eaten the right breakfast? Hired the right piano teacher?

No, I had the right formula for a flawless performance, except for one thing—delight. I think the only thing that could have made a difference for me in that moment was to have a greater love for the music I was playing than my fear of what others thought of me. I froze because I cared more about the execution than the experience. The *what* over the *why*. The *how*

I look over the *who I am*. I was so focused on not messing up that I missed the reason why a pianist ought to play a complex étude in the first place: for the love of music.

You might not be a concert pianist, but I'm guessing you, too, know how it feels to be so consumed by the pressure to perform that you miss the significance of purpose and delight in the very things you've been given to do.

It happens when we're so focused on whether our kids are saying and doing all the right things that we forget how much they need us to pursue their hearts.

Or when we excitedly check off the box next to each day's Bible reading plan but don't know how anything we've read really applies to our lives.

When we'd rather sign up for a volunteer job at church than spend an hour in prayer with the Lord.

When we've worked and worked to clean up our lives or our image but quickly forget who we are in the face of fear and doubt.

You may remember the infamous words of Olympic gold medalist Eric Liddell. He said of his running: "[God] made me fast. And when I run, I feel his pleasure."[1] I don't know what pressures he faced, but I do know that these are the words of a man who loved doing what he was created to do. He experienced closeness with God as a result of simply enjoying God's gifting in his life, not his achievements through it. It seems poignant that he didn't cite winning as God's pleasure with him, but simply running. Do you see it? Medaling wasn't the mark of God's favor. Doing what he was made by God to do felt like God's delight.

If I'm honest, God's delight and desire for me to experience his presence rarely crosses my mind when I've got a job to do. I'm usually too concerned with whether I'll mess up or how well I'll perform. Truth is, I can't think about God's pleasure and provision through the way he made me when I'm more focused on what others think of me. You can't long for the approval of God *and* others at the same time. One always eclipses the other.

I wonder how many times I've forfeited freedom in doing what God's called me to do because I've been more aware of my performance than God's purpose in creating me for the task. I'm sure too many to count. And perhaps for you too.

What is something God's given you to do?

Does the approval of others keep you from responding in faith?

Are you more concerned with your performance or God's presence in doing the work?

When I substitute God's purpose with my own performance, I make myself a slave to perfection, believing my awesomeness will save me from discomfort, embarrassment, and other fears I dread most. And when I let myself believe that my performance is the key to securing all that I need in life, including God's favor, I set myself up for joyless doing.

Speaking of joyless doing, the Pharisees of Jesus' day had their performance nailed down but were known as some of the most joyless, judgmental people in Jewish culture. Fear, not freedom, was the Pharisee motto. Fear of not measuring up, fear of not doing it right, fear of performing poorly—the Pharisees made sure they instilled these fears in all who sought to understand the way to God through them. They were consumed with appearing righteous and eager to flaunt their perfect execution of the Law. They had taken the Law of God and added their own ideas, their own requirements.

So when, in Matthew 15, the Pharisees sought to trap Jesus as a lawbreaker, Jesus exposed them with words prophesied by Isaiah. "This people honors me with their lips, but their heart is far from me; in vain do they worship me, teaching as doctrines the commandments of men" (vv. 8–9).

In other words, the Pharisees said the right things, acted according to the rules, and appeared to honor God. They were religious (maybe even what we'd consider "good Christians" in our day based on appearances) but cared more about their performance than God's true pleasure in and with them. They were driven by public consumption rather than private consecration, and Jesus knew he didn't have their hearts. Adherence and execution minus love equals joyless religiosity.

Without love, our acts of faith are but a production—a show. Deliverance, according to the Pharisees, came through following rules. Their striving was about themselves, not God. If it had been about Jesus, they wouldn't have repackaged manmade rules as God's commands.

If taking an honest look at the picture-perfect performance of the Pharisees wrecks you in the places no one sees deep in your heart, you're not alone. It should. Their lip-service-sans-heart-surrender ways still linger with us today. How often do we look to performance as our true hope . . .

- when we care more about our kids behaving a certain way in public,
- when we're eager to snap a pic of our quiet time for social media,
- when we struggle to give in secret, or
- when we don't let others into our struggles with sin.

When we work to preserve the picture of our performance, we miss the very point of the gospel. Jesus offered deliverance through dependence on him. The Pharisees taught deliverance through dependence on perfection and performance.

Friend, performance over presence—God's presence—always leaves us fearfully reliant on our perfect execution rather than Christ's perfect deliverance. If you're weary and tired of managing your performance, you're in good company.

Our Hero Complexes

I don't know your background with the church or your relationship with Jesus, but I want you to know that, if you've been given a gospel of striving—a gospel of Jesus plus performance and a whole bunch of other stuff—you've not experienced the true gospel of grace through Jesus alone. Perhaps you've been told that you must look a certain way, act in a specific manner, or perform to a certain standard in order to come to Christ. That's simply untrue and is a false gospel akin to that of the Pharisees. And when a gospel promotes striving in your own strength, it isn't good news at all.

But, friend, if alternatively you've been given a gospel that downplays holiness and obedience, eliminates God's sovereign ways, and antiquates the law-satisfying work of the cross of Christ, you've been fed another version of a gospel of striving. Just because the striving is not religious or devout, or does not include churchy work, doesn't mean it's not still striving. Our current cultural idea of salvation through our merit (even in the church!) finds itself rooted less in "good works" and more

Performance over presence—God's presence—always leaves us fearfully reliant on our perfect execution rather than Christ's perfect deliverance.

in self-improvement and self-love. If ancient-world Phariseeism added more religious rules to God's Law as a means of salvation, modern Western Phariseeism replaces God's Law—fulfilled God's way—with self-made laws fulfilled in self-satisfying ways. We've become our own heroes—the saviors to our own stories.

Pleasing yourself doesn't sound like burdensome striving, but that's the lie the Enemy wants you to believe. That is the false gospel of this generation—that we can save ourselves through ourselves. That with enough practice, enough resources, and enough work, a perfectly executed version of your life is accessible. This generation is declaring: Be your own boss and make yourself happy! Save yourself!

While this self-reliant way of salvation denies an absolute standard for truth or goodness, it declares *absolutely* that the truth resides within ourselves. It baffles me that our culture is obsessed with the contradictions of this ideology and equates them with freedom.

Is discovering your own truth truly as freeing as we're led to believe? Is being the hero of your own story actually a relief? Is self-reliance truly satisfying? Does constantly keeping your finger to the wind promote rest or worry? Can you be perfect enough to ensure happiness?

Just my personal observation: being your own hero doesn't seem all that freeing; it looks exhausting.

It seems the constant obsession with appointing ourselves the heroes of our own lives is catching up with us. We're practically hooked up to our self-bettering resources intravenously, so dependent on the latest content in books, podcasts, webinars, and more that we think continually about ourselves: *Who am I?*

Being your own
hero doesn't seem
all that freeing;
it looks
exhausting.

What's my purpose? How do I belong? Am I enough? Does anyone love me? There's nothing wrong with these questions; the answers just were never meant to be found within ourselves.

In an interview for *GQ*, Danish psychologist Svend Brinkmann pointed out that our "self-help craze, the imperative to perform and be flexible and optimize yourself all the time" has become pathological, with us becoming victims of self-optimization fatigue. He pinpointed the problem with self-betterment and the exhausting pursuit of arriving at the finish line of your best self, saying, "It's a process without end. . . . if we're only okay as long as we are striving, moving, developing, then we're never okay."[2] We want to feel okay. We want to be enough. We want to arrive at the finish line as the winners. And we keep believing we can make it happen if we just optimize our performance and carry it out flawlessly.

I feel a GraceLaced hand-lettered art print coming on: *Jesus is the hero of your story.* (Wink.)

And, quite frankly, he is. But Jesus didn't seek to be a hero; he simply sought to be faithful. Jesus didn't try to steal the show, improve on God's plan of salvation with addendum or flair, or demand honor for the Savior he was. At every turn, Jesus wanted only to do what the Father purposed for him to do. No more, no less. Even as he faced brutal death on the cross, Jesus revealed his motivation in staying faithful to the work he'd been given. It was not in pursuit of showing himself worthy or becoming his best self. It was . . .

- **to do God's will and not his own.** "Father, if you are willing, remove this cup from me. Nevertheless, not my will, but yours, be done" (Luke 22:42).

- *to glorify God and not himself.* "Father, the hour has come; glorify your Son that the Son may glorify you" (John 17:1).
- *that we might know that everything is from God.* "Now they know that everything that you have given me is from you" (John 17:7).
- *that we might know God's love.* "I made known to them your name, and I will continue to make it known, that the love with which you have loved me may be in them, and I in them" (John 17:26).

This is an example that is hard to follow, especially for all of us who have spent so long subscribing to the hero narrative we've been taught. But it is one worth mulling over as we seek a more genuine and faithful way forward.

Not Slipping Up

My boys have taken an interest in dirt biking and Supercross racing. (Listen—when I say I'm an unlikely mom to six boys, I mean it.) I didn't expect to have such a vested interest in the sport, but I do. I know—I'm surprised too. For a woman who considers sunset-chasing and hunting for the best deals on any sales rack competitive sports, watching Supercross races and catching myself screaming at the television screen for my favorite racer to cross the finish line is just, well, unexpected.

Supercross is an individual sport; each rider is responsible for executing the perfect line of attack all the way to the checkered flag. The goal and strategy, I've learned, is to get out in front of the pack right away, then maintain your position by calculating every turn, every rut, every whoop or triple jump, meticulously. (Sisters, you still with me?)

The key to maintaining your position is to not slip up, to not slow your speed, to never let down your guard. It's a nail-biter to watch but even more intense to be the rider who stands to lose it all if he doesn't keep up.

I can't help but think of my sisters, full throttle, looking for the fastest line that will ensure them a place at the podium.

We are straining to get ahead. We are striving for perfect execution. We are attempting to foresee any obstacles or complications. We are working to save ourselves.

Read that formula for success again: *the key to maintaining your position is to not slip up.* I don't know about you, but I'm worn out just reading those words. Slipping up is my specialty. And trying to avoid it is my continual pursuit. Unless my place is secure apart from my performance.

Jesus' agenda was God's agenda. His only finish line was the one God the Father ordained for him. Love, delight, and oneness defined the perfect unity between Jesus and the Father—no wonder Jesus was unstoppable and undeterred in carrying out the work God purposed for him. And here's the secret to our doing the same, following in his steps:

"I in them and you in me, that they may become perfectly one, so that the world may know that you sent me and loved them even as you loved me" (John 17:23).

We are invited into the perfect unity between God the Father and God the Son. That was the plan all along. God's plan of redemption brings us back into intimate relationship and unhindered fellowship with him so that we no longer have to carve the perfect path for ourselves through striving. Saving performance addicts like me and you, striving to earn our place in the kingdom with self-made perfection: that's what the death, burial, and resurrection of Christ accomplished.

Driven by Delight

My third son wanders off to the piano in the living room each night after the dinner dishes are put away. With piano lessons halted at the start of COVID-19, he plays some older music assigned to him and the rest he plays by ear. From the other room I hear him get beautiful notes right and so many notes wrong. I've been known to occasionally call out, "B-flat, Judah! That's supposed to be a B-flat." But he is unfazed and fearless, absorbed in the love of melody as he tinkers on. He's not playing to perform; he's playing for the love of music. He doesn't look around to the right or left, and he isn't trying to be the best. Regardless of whether he finds himself on a stage one day, I can't help but take note: this is what it looks like to be driven by delight and not the pressure to perform. How much better we play and how much more we desire to stay when we feel God's delight in what he's called us to do.

I pray you stay. I pray you know his delight in and through you. I pray you know you can't save yourself, no matter how well you perform. There's hope for me, and there's hope for you. God's good gifts don't depend on your perfection; they've already been secured in our perfect Savior, Christ. The pressure's off, friend. Get off that stage, and rest.

SIX

The Lunchroom

Striving to Belong

*I am not my own, but belong—body and soul,
in life and death—to my faithful Savior, Jesus
Christ.*

—HEIDELBERG CATECHISM

t was 1981, and my newly immigrated parents trusted my kindergarten sense of awareness enough to concede to a Strawberry Shortcake metal lunchbox, the kind that felt like a topographical map depicting an adventure with her assorted confectionary friends. I was so proud of that lunchbox. With the Strawberry Shortcake lunchbox in hand, I felt prepared for anything—the language barrier, confusion over what was funny and what was not funny, comments about the shape of my eyes, and the inevitable get-to-know-you game of asking me to interpret what *ching-chong-ding-dong* meant in Chinese.

But I wasn't prepared for the lunchroom.

No truer words have ever been written about school lunches than these from Anne Lamott:

> Here is the main thing I know about public school lunches: it only *looked* like a bunch of kids eating lunch. It was really about opening our insides in front of everyone. . . . The contents of your lunch said whether or not you and your family were Okay. . . .
>
> Your sandwich was the centerpiece, and there were strict guidelines. It almost goes without saying that store-bought white bread was the only acceptable bread.[1]

This was my exact experience in the elementary school cafeteria. My parents didn't know about Rainbo white bread. They weren't accustomed to buying peanut butter and grape jelly. They didn't get the memo on the bologna and sliced American cheese combo that declared to all that your mom and dad were normal, that they were upper- to middle-class Americans with a minivan, and that they *belonged*.

My parents showed their love, resourcefulness, and belonging by packing a cleaned-out and reused Dannon yogurt container with the previous night's dinner of fried rice. Before we move on any further, I feel it's practically a public service announcement for us to talk about fried rice real quick. (If we haven't formally met, my name is Ruth—wannabe cooking show host.) Fried rice is the simplest, most satisfying way to get your Chinese food fix with what you might already have in your fridge: old cooked rice, onions, chopped precooked meat or deli meat, eggs, frozen or fresh veggies, soy sauce, oil, a big squirt of sriracha, whatever it is that you have handy. You can get fancy, but this will get you a Chinese meal in one bowl. And like a Chinese mom, I don't really have measurements and details for how I like to make it; just come over and watch me do it. Oil, eggs, onions, meat, veggies, rice, soy sauce, fish sauce if you're inclined, pepper, a sprinkle of sugar, a little sesame oil, some chili sauce—it's *easy*. And this life tip will serve you well: chop or dice all your meats and veggies into comparable sizes. And taste, taste, taste. That's it.

As well-received as fried rice is now, it was a different story when I was a kid. Apparently, by the reaction of other kids in the lunchroom, my parents made our beloved fried rice with something that caused it to look or smell like slimy frogs who ate mold. The wincing, nose-pinching, gawking, and horror of a Dannon yogurt container that did not contain strawberry yogurt! Gasp. It was unthinkable, and I was suddenly, decidedly, effectively declared an outsider. I did not belong.

Yogurt companies the world over must have also gotten word of my lunchroom faux pas, as I've seen a distinct lack of lids and reusability in individual yogurt containers. Just saying.

I wanted so badly to be accepted in a new country, to really actually enjoy bologna, to avoid the whispering behind my back and the letter on my chest that let everyone know I was the outsider. Who knew the contents of your lunch could reveal, like the headline of every paper in every newsstand, "You don't belong"?

Of course, it's funny to me now. Of course, my adult friends beg me to make fried rice for lunch when they come over to hang out these days. (And, oh yes, I add fish sauce.) Of course, it doesn't look or smell like slimy frogs who eat mold. And I know I'm biased, but of course fried rice is more appealing than white bread and processed meat slices. Of course, we know lunchroom conformity isn't true belonging.

Or do we?

If only bringing the right lunch secured the belonging we're all looking for. We know it doesn't. But, truth is, we live as though it might.

I'm writing this chapter from the sixth month of our country's fight against a global pandemic. If you were online at all in the first half of 2020, you may have felt both more connected than ever to the internet, with this global shift to socially distanced *everything* (learning, relationships, celebrations, church, employment) and equally disillusioned at online life entirely.

If you were on social media at all the first half of 2020, you likely questioned your *belonging*.

The early months of 2020 were marked by angst and heartache around the globe, but specifically in the United States, cities experienced social unrest, protests, and anger over racial injustices, worldview clashes, and a difference in social ideologies. It felt as if everyone was yelling all the time on the internet. The outrage about multiple issues across social and media platforms drew lines of separation between anyone who thought differently than you. While my most meaningful conversations about hard topics always happened around my kitchen table with people in my home and in my community, I still felt swallowed up in the fear of being misjudged, misunderstood, labeled, or canceled. Belonging was easily the commodity of choice in 2020, as people banded together with like-minded folks, finding safety within their own arenas of thought.

I found myself anxious and distraught—understandable in light of so many burdens of this season, but at the core of the distress was a deep desire to belong. I noticed my loss of appetite, knots in my shoulders, butterflies in my stomach, and daily headaches—all because I had been trained to define, determine, and check in on my sense of belonging according to the unrelenting pace of the internet. If my body wasn't telling the full story of my ill-placed longing for belonging, my thoughts certainly were. A middle-aged mom of many, who likely knows herself better now than she did twenty years ago and writes and shares her perspective for a living, still struggling with belonging? Yes, it surprised me too.

In our heightened reliance on digital platforms for connectedness, we've all felt the pressure to live out and declare our most intimate and even our not-yet-fully-formed convictions, opinions, and preferences—right now, today; *yesterday* would've been better.

Yes, the collective—the weight of group think—can be used for good or for evil. Yes, it is undoubtedly a privilege to use any and all influence we have with those right in front of us and those we have access to globally. But I wonder if we're looking for belonging in all the wrong places—and paying too high a price with the wrong currency.

Brené Brown has famously written lots of lovely things about the subject with highly quotable and meme-able conclusions, such as: "true belonging only happens when we present our authentic, imperfect selves to the world, our sense of belonging can never be greater than our level of self-acceptance."[2]

To be known and loved—that's what we are longing for when we look for belonging. And Brené Brown is not wrong when she

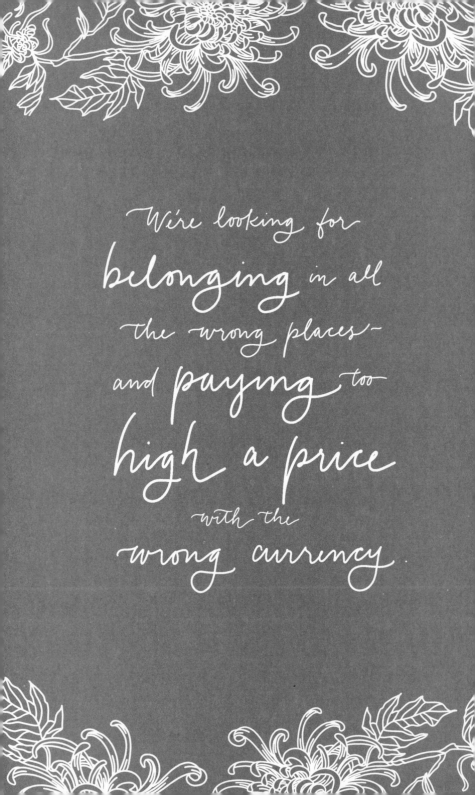

We're looking for
belonging in all
the wrong places—
and *paying* too
high a price
with the
wrong currency.

calls on courage and vulnerability as the conduit for authentic impact. But what if—whether you're looking for belonging in the year 2020 or the year AD 20—belonging isn't meant to be found within yourself or with others?

The answer to the first question of the Heidelberg Catechism shapes a definition of belonging that doesn't rely on self-imaging, self-improvement, or anyone else's input but the Savior's:

Q. What is your only comfort in life and in death?

A. That I am not my own, but belong—body and soul, in
   life and in death—to my faithful Savior, Jesus Christ.
   He has fully paid for all my sins with his precious blood,
   and has set me free from the tyranny of the devil. He
   also watches over me in such a way that not a hair
   can fall from my head without the will of my Father
   in heaven; in fact, all things must work together for
   my salvation. Because I belong to him, Christ, by his
   Holy Spirit, assures me of eternal life and makes me
   wholeheartedly willing and ready from now on to live
   for him.[3]

The writers of the catechism didn't have to find their words through their feelings—their words were all found in Scripture. Turns out the Bible has much to say about our belonging.

- I am not my own. (1 Cor. 6:19–20)
- I am his in life or death. (Rom. 14:7–9)
- I belong to Christ, and Christ belongs to God.
  (1 Cor. 3:23)
- I am purchased and paid for. (1 Peter 1:18–19)

- I am set free. (John 8:34–36)
- I am safe and secure. (John 10:27–30)
- I am intimately cared for. (Matt. 10:29–31)
- God purposes all things for my good. (Rom. 8:28)
- I am forever sealed and secured in him. (Eph. 1:13–14)
- I'm enabled to live by the Spirit. (Rom. 8:1–17)

We were made *by* God and *for* God, so is it any wonder that Christ followers find belonging *in* God?

Belonging in itself isn't the prize—how can it be? It's what belonging offers that we long for: the unshakeable comfort and assurance that we are known and loved.

Our self-acceptance, then, according to God's Word, isn't something we will discover with enough self-love but is rather an extension of the work of redemption in our lives when we discover how much God loves *us*. We were made to belong to Jesus first. Not to religious affiliation, political parties, justice movements, or social circles. We don't even primarily belong to our children, parents, churches, or spouses.

I've been known to cheekily introduce myself, when Troy and I are meeting new people, in this way: "I'm Ruth—I belong to Troy." Saying so conveys affection but also that I am happily knit together with this man that I love—I'm *with* someone I've committed to. As much as it affectionately conveys our marriage bond when Troy and I say we "belong" to each other, when we're talking of belonging to Jesus, marriage is but a shadow, an imperfect picture, of the greater, deeper bond we were made for in Christ.

This is the belonging Jesus meant when he spoke of his relationship to God the Father in John 17 as we read in the last chapter. It's what the apostle Paul meant when he said, "to live is Christ" (Phil. 1:21). And what he meant when he said in his letter to the Corinthians:

> Do you not know that your bodies are temples of the Holy Spirit, who is in you, whom you have received from God? You are not your own; you were bought at a price. Therefore honor God with your bodies. (1 Cor. 6:19–20 NIV)

You are not your own; you were bought at a price. Huh? Paul's got my attention. This doesn't sound like the Christianity that is currently packing stadiums, filling seats at celebrity-clad Sunday services, or printed onto decorative pillows across America. This kind of belonging is not convenient association and leaves no room for living for yourself. In Christ, belonging isn't mere affection, camaraderie, or membership in the same club, as it can seem in mainstream Christianity. It is so much more.

The price of our belonging was set and met through the sacrifice of God's son, Jesus Christ, our redeemer. The word *redeemed* means just that: to gain possession of something through payment. That's why Paul said we are not our own. God loves us so much that he rescued us from the grip of anything else that promises to satisfy, and instead he made us belong to him alone. This is a costly, sacrificial, all-out rescue from the slave market of sin to the household of God.

When we don't remember that we were made to be God's possessions, and what it cost for us to be his, we end up longing for belonging everywhere else. Through the clothes we wear, the people we engage, the work we do—we look for home in identifiers rather than our identities in Christ. But most conveniently,

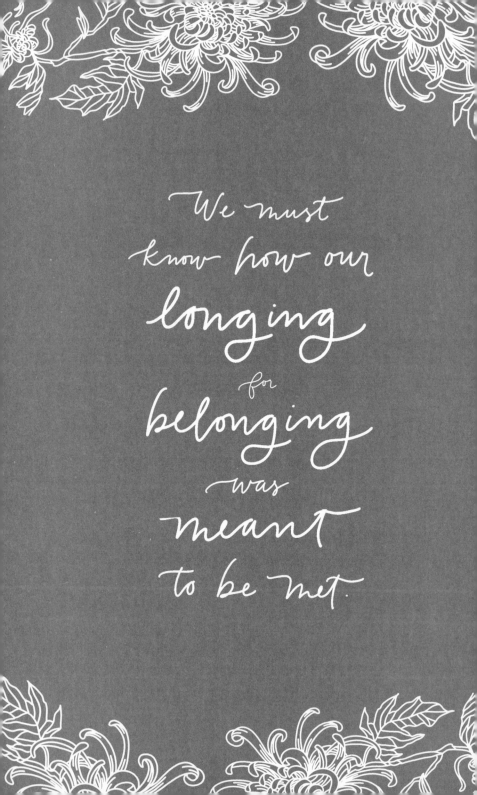

We must
know how our
longing
for
belonging
was
meant
to be met.

we turn to the homes found within our phones—giving our devices our mental focus, monetary resources, and our best hours each day.

We can use our phones and not be bossed by them. We can participate on social media and not be ruled by its messages for or about us. We can invest deeply in relationships in our homes and around the world without making those people stand in the place of God in our lives.

We can, but we must first know how our longing for belonging was meant to be met. We must know who we belong to.

Without knowing the biblically informed answers to the overarching question of where we find comfort in life and death, even good things—like elementary school lunches, loving spouses, ministries, cell phones, and friendship—become whips that drive us to better fit ourselves within a mold. Without knowing our belonging in Jesus, we will strive to belong as our highest hope—in groups, among peers, with family, at church.

In Christ, on the other hand, we've been fit and fashioned for the belonging we were always made for. We're not working tirelessly and endlessly to somehow become a version of ourselves that is more desirable or acceptable to some unachievable standard. We are not slaves to a cruel master of social approval or popular opinion but gratefully mastered by a loving Father.

When we are in Christ, we are simply aware of who we belong to first and foremost. And, friend, that's when we can let go of all the world tells us to do in order to belong. Because we are already seen, known, rescued, and loved.

SEVEN

Honor and Shame

Striving to Outrun Shame

*For I am convinced that neither death nor life,
neither angels nor demons, neither the present
nor the future, nor any powers, neither height
nor depth, nor anything else in all creation, will
be able to separate us from the love of God that
is in Christ Jesus our Lord.*

—ROMANS 8:38–39 NIV

I've been dreading this chapter. It's the one that feels most unfinished and unresolved in my life—not in a lack of theological understanding sense but, rather, in the way that, when a wound is not yet fully recovered, it easily finds itself exposed and raw when the scab is inadvertently scraped off. Then the healing process must begin again.

That's what my relationship with shame is like. I don't mean shame like the regret of living a duplicitous life as a teen—wanting to honor the Lord, while making excuses for dishonorable behavior in secret. I also don't mean the shame that accompanied that one name I was called by a family member in a fit of anger. I'm talking about the kind of shame that rifles through your pantry, makes dinner for himself, and stays all night, chattering away without invitation, leaving messes to clean up and dirty shoe markings on the table where he carelessly leaned back in his chair and overstayed his welcome.

Shame, by definition, is a painful emotion caused by consciousness of guilt, shortcoming, or wrongdoing. Biblically, it's what Adam and Eve felt when they sinned and hid from God. Before sin and the awareness of their own sin, they felt no shame (Gen. 3). Shame entered when God's commands were questioned and deemed not enough. And when I look at my life, I see it too: when I go searching for better, self-betterment, or a better position with others than what God has given, my discontentment leads me away from satisfaction—to shame.

Stay with me, friend. Don't check out right now if you don't have a list of regrets or humiliating moments (wait—you don't?). I'm wanting us to look at so much more than just a bad track record. I want us to think about the ways in which we all deal with deep-seated shame and how our striving proves our efforts to run from it.

Dr. Curt Thompson insightfully helped us look at a more nuanced shade of shame in this way:

By shame I am not talking about something that necessarily requires the intensity of extreme humiliation. Rather, it is born out of a sense of "there being something wrong" with me or of "not being enough" and therefore exudes the aroma of being unable or powerless to change one's condition or circumstances.[1]

Yes, *that.*

In other words, shame isn't just feeling unworthy over something you should or shouldn't have done but rather the nagging feeling that no matter what you do or don't do, you'll never get it right. Not enough. Forever lacking. Fundamentally incapable of being who others expect or hope you'll be. That's the shame I know intimately, privately—spelled out in verbal and nonverbal ways by some of the people I've loved the most.

I feel as if I've known shame—and the accompanying need to either prove my worthiness or outrun my feelings of inadequacy—my whole life. My guess is that you've known something of this kind of shame as well. Maybe your family is too proud to admit it. Maybe your church is too fearful to address it. Maybe your friends are too distracted to work through it. Maybe you're too weary to face it.

Without the hope of honor—or true shame replacement—shame can either leave us feeling condemned or anxiously striving to outrun its consuming effect on our lives.

For Asian Americans, the honor-shame mentality runs deep within the fabric of our cultural values. The simple solution for someone influenced by Asian cultural norms is to believe honor prevents (notice: not absolves) shame. So, there's a perpetual running after honor and a perpetual escaping of shame. Even though I was raised mostly in the States, I knew the importance of *mianzi*—literally "face" or "giving face." It's a cultural pheno-menon that seeks to award favor by acting in accordance with hierarchy or reputation. You either have face, or you lose face by dishonoring someone who is due respect from you, or simply by not living up to societal standards. *Mianzi* is so important that all Asian mothers prewarn their children whom to serve first at dinner, how to address each person present, what denotes respect, and what behavior would cause the family deep shame and a loss of face—*diu lian*.

These two simple words didn't simply mean, quite literally, "lose face." Said with enough bite, the phrase was condemna-tion you couldn't easily recover from. In Chinese culture, *diu lian* is not just doing something humiliating but being someone who causes humiliation to others as well. Do you remember the song from Disney's 1998 version of *Mulan*, "Bring Honor to Us All"? It's that, but the opposite. *Diu lian* is the very essence of not meeting another's expectation for your behavior, reputation, or choices.

Even something as seemingly insignificant as who pays the bill at a meal is of monumental concern for Asians. I've witnessed a few arm wrestling matches, some incredible footwork, impres-sive agility, and great lengths taken to beat out a friend or relative to the front cash register at a restaurant. It can be a serious part of dinner—the long and arduous game of keep-away with the bill. All to appropriately give *mianzi* to others or to save face yourself. When it's this culturally important to publicly show honor or prove your integrity before a watching world (whether you really want to pay the bill or not), it's no surprise that fear, anxiety, pride, and people-pleasing begin to dominate motives.

If we're honest, we recognize that idea of outrunning shame isn't so much just an Eastern idea. It's a humanity issue.

Since I'm writing these pages from the socially distanced, virtually charged days of a global crisis and virtue signaling, I can't help but think of the rise of cancel culture this year in the United States *all over the internet.* While our Western culture notoriously maintains a fierce claim on individual thought and freedoms, this year has felt different. It's felt more akin to the cultural norms of my youth and familial community; the collective now reigns.

Social media posts, brand alignment, political affiliation, mask wearing, vaccines, protests, news channels. These are just a few areas where the collective is now shaping what we think of as acceptable. The sad part is the way we've come to determine someone's worthiness based on our different definitions of acceptability. We've somehow replaced identity with identification. We've bought into the paradigm that our "faces"—or *Face*book pages, rather—are the summation of who we are.

Identification instead of identity. Condemnation or an attempt to outrun it. These are the ideals we've seemingly allowed ourselves to operate under.

Neighbors shocked and disappointed in folks they've grilled burgers with for years. Friends unfriending friends over political posts. Brands dropped over email rhetoric. Family members not speaking to one another over assumptions made from a Share button. Leaders experiencing loss of impact by speaking too soon or not soon enough.

I'm guessing you get it. While we may not hold important government offices, be Hollywood celebrities, or have millions of followers, we've felt the weight, fear, and confusion of this intense shift in modern impact: apparently, we *are* what we do or don't do publicly.

In this East-meets-West moment, our identities are defined by the identifications of honor or shame we bring to our communities.

Abdu Murray pointed out in his timely insights on this topic:

> In cancel culture, a single mistake is perpetually unforgivable because it's not simply a guilty *act*. Rather, the mistake defines the individual's identity, turning them into a shameful *person*—someone who can be "canceled."[2]

I think that is what we find so shocking and overwhelming about the cancel culture of our present day—there are no second chances in a worldview whose standard is its own, made up by a collective that determines what it won't tolerate and what it will. When the moral standard is changing and disconnected from a source of authority, those who don't measure up get left behind. The goal of cancel culture isn't to redeem, restore, or reconcile; it is to reprimand.

Shamed into the preferred behavior is a familiar feeling for many of us. A mother's anger, a father's silence, a friend or colleague who believes the worst about you based on hearsay—you can feel canceled in a lot of ways in your everyday life.

Shaming is manipulation, and manipulation is, by definition, controlling or influencing someone using cunning, unfair means—means that make the perpetrator the one above all others. Do you see why shaming is, therefore, not neutral—but sinful?

When we seek to control others through wielding the power

of shame, we are telling God that he is not enough to make wrong right. We are telling him that he's not capable enough to change another's heart. We are believing those lies when we try to manipulate our *own way* out of shame as well. How do we do this? Tim Keller put it this way:

> Religious persons obey to get leverage over God, to control him, to put him in a position where they think he owes them. Therefore, despite their moral and religious fastidiousness, they are actually attempting to be their own saviors. Christians, who know they are only saved by grace and can never control God, obey him out of a desire to love and please and draw closer to the one who saved them.[3]

Whether you are looking for true biblical change or change that is self-serving, I want to offer this gentle reminder: we were never meant to be the Holy Spirit. He is God, and we are not.

If unchecked against the true character of God and our true identity in Christ, our self-reliance and pride will cause us to resort to shaming and manipulation. And, similarly, if unchecked against the true character of God and our true identity in Christ, our self-condemning shame and feelings of inadequacy will keep us from drawing near—from coming home—to the Lord.

Truth is, striving to outrun shame is a legitimate option for someone who thinks she can position herself to always be one step ahead of feeling unworthy. She may believe, *If I just get that promotion, I won't feel like such a failure,* or *If I just make myself attractive enough, others won't see how ugly I feel.* It's possible to avoid feeling shame with a lot of maneuvering and sidestepping, but eventually, we all get tired of running.

He is God,
and
we are not.

We weren't meant to live this way. Sometimes we just don't see how much we're striving until we see how worn out we are from trying to attain something God wants to give us through himself.

Have you been running, friend? Have you felt hurt and canceled in some intimate places in your life? Have you messed up so much there appears to be no recovering? Maybe you've been dismissed publicly. Abandoned at your nadir. Relationally canceled before you even had a chance to prove the inaccuracy of what was said about you.

And maybe you, too, have wished for grace.

Grace for your inadequacies. Grace for your mistakes. Grace for when you've made everyone proud. And grace for when everyone wants to look away. Grace for the shame you've blocked out. Grace for the shame that lingers. Grace for right now. Grace for what hasn't even happened yet.

My desire is not just to help you to cease striving but to replace empty striving with the fulfillment we are all looking for. When we strive to avoid shame, the antidote isn't self-love—that's where I think current self-help fails us as Christ followers. We don't need to simply feel no shame; instead, we need to recognize that the entire redemption story is about shame and "everything Scripture says about shame converges at Jesus. From his birth to his crucifixion, the shame of the world was distilled to its most concentrated form and washed over him."[4]

Even greater than our attempts to outrun the feeling of shame and inadequacy is the length to which God has taken our shame, bestowed honor on us, and canceled our debts.

Jesus spoke into this when he told parables illustrating key principles and truths about God and salvation to an Eastern, visual, and verbal culture—a culture that operated out of the honor and shame mentality we in the West only now are coming to know. Of all the stories Jesus told, the parable of the prodigal son is perhaps the most beloved. Turn to Luke 15:11–32 with me.

There was a man who had two sons. And the younger of them said to his father, "Father, give me the share of property that is coming to me." And he divided his property between them. Not many days later, the younger son gathered all he had and took a journey into a far country, and there he squandered his property in reckless living. And when he had spent everything, a severe famine arose in that country, and he began to be in need. So he went and hired himself out to one of the citizens of that country, who sent him into his fields to feed pigs. And he was longing to be fed with the pods that the pigs ate, and no one gave him anything.

But when he came to himself, he said, "How many of my father's hired servants have more than enough bread, but I perish here with hunger! I will arise and go to my father, and I will say to him, 'Father, I have sinned against heaven and before you. I am no longer worthy to be called your son. Treat me as one of your hired servants.'" And he arose and came to his father. But while he was still a long way off, his father saw him and felt compassion, and ran and embraced him and kissed him. And the son said to him, "Father, I have sinned against heaven and before you. I am no longer worthy to be called your son." But the father said to his servants, "Bring quickly the best robe, and put it on him, and put a ring on his hand, and shoes on his feet. And bring the fattened calf and kill it, and let us eat and celebrate. For this my son was dead, and is alive again; he was lost, and is found." And they began to celebrate.

Now his older son was in the field, and as he came and drew near to the house, he heard music and dancing. And he called one of the servants and asked what these things meant. And he said to him, "Your brother has come, and your father has killed the fattened calf, because he has received him back safe and sound." But he was angry and refused to go in. His father came out and entreated him, but he answered his father, "Look, these many years I have served you, and I never disobeyed your command, yet you never gave me a young goat, that I might celebrate with my friends. But when this son of yours came, who has devoured your property with prostitutes, you killed the fattened calf for him!" And he said to him, "Son, you are always with me, and all that is mine is yours. It was fitting to celebrate and be glad, for this your brother was dead, and is alive; he was lost, and is found."

Jesus told this parable in the setting of Pharisees whispering and complaining about Jesus for lacking conformity to their self-righteous standards, while the sinners and tax collectors gathered around to hear him teach. Jesus told this parable to hold up a mirror, and I think we can let it do the same for us, these thousands of years later. We often think this parable is about God's love and restoration of us, the shamed sinners. But it's equally about God's exhortation to us, the self-righteous shamers. There are two brothers in this story: the one who has been shameful, and the one who is striving to outrun shame.

Books and sermon series have been written on this parable,

and I won't seek to say everything there is to say about it here, but what I want you to notice is:

- It was shameful to ask for your inheritance before the death of a parent.
- It was shameful to squander what was entrusted to you.
- It was shameful to live with pigs, the symbol of uncleanness.
- It was shameful to return so unworthy to your father.

But here's the shocking thing that comes next: "But while he was still a long way off, his father saw him and felt compassion, and ran and embraced him and kissed him" (v. 20).

A Middle Eastern man in the first century did not run. This is fascinating to me as I read more background and historical context for this parable. We have to understand these words that Jesus spoke in the context of his audience at the time. Ever heard the phrase, *gird your loins*? Well, that's exactly what a Middle Eastern man of the first century would have had to do in order to run. And in doing so, he would have inevitably shown his bare legs. This was considered shameful and unacceptable in Jewish culture.

The listeners of this parable, if not already mortified at the younger son's behavior, now likely responded to the father's behavior with even greater disgust.

Before we get to why the father did this shocking thing and ran to his son, let me share one more incredible historical detail of significance that gives so much insight to this parable.

Kezazah is a ceremony in Jewish culture that was performed when a Jewish boy lost his inheritance to Gentiles. The ceremony literally meant to be cut off (like "canceled"). Upon his shameful return, the older men of the community would meet the younger man at the city gates and throw a pot down onto the ground, signifying the broken relationship and the state of being cut off from his family. A young Jewish male who lost his wealth to a Gentile would not be allowed to return to the community. The father was expected to sit, emotionally detached, in his home while the community—the collective—formally deemed the son unworthy.[5]

So why, then, would the father in this parable run to greet his son? While we undoubtedly read into the text an understandable motivation of love and earnest joy in seeing the son's return, historical context would suggest that the father ran in order to save his son, to redeem his son before the *kezazah* ceremony could even occur. He preemptively rescued his sinful son by bearing shame himself.

Just pause.

Let that sink in. Go grab a cup of tea, and meet me back here after you've let that steep a little. I'll wait.

You back? Okay.

Sister, the antidote to our obsession with striving—and specifically, striving to outrun the shame we fear—is open-arms surrender to a Father who takes the shame meant for us and makes us worthy of forgiveness and love. Notice I didn't say "finds us worthy of forgiveness and love." The father of the prodigal son didn't find him in that condition—he chose and declared him so. He made *himself* a spectacle. He absorbed the humiliation meant for his child.

So make no mistake, this is not a fluffy promise found in self-affirmation or self-love; it is anchored in what Scripture says about God's love, God's rescue, God's provision, and God's work to make us right—justified—with him and his honor:

> Therefore, since we have been justified by faith, we have peace with God through our Lord Jesus Christ. Through him we have also obtained access by faith into this grace in which we stand, and we rejoice in hope of the glory of God. Not only that, but we rejoice in our sufferings, knowing that suffering produces endurance, and endurance produces character, and character produces hope, and hope does not put us to shame, because God's love has been poured into our hearts through the Holy Spirit who has been given to us. (Rom. 5:1–5)

God does not cancel you, but comforts you in your shame.

God does not shame you, but Christ bears your shame.

God does not stand far off in judgment but runs to you in welcome.

Okay, but what about the older brother? The story doesn't end with the father's embrace—and the replacement of the *kezazah* ceremony with a feast; it ends with a bitter older brother.

Remember, this isn't an illustration about one kind of sinner, but two. Again, who was Jesus telling this parable to? He was addressing those who thought themselves holy by never breaking the Law and those who saw themselves as hopeless because they'd broken it over and over again. Jesus told this parable to show that both were alienated as lawbreakers, both were given access to the Father, and both could be forgiven partakers of all that is Christ's.

The difference between the two sons—the difference between those of us who try to outrun our shame and those of us who repent of the sin that caused it in the first place—can be seen in the older brother's response to his brother's repentance and the father's welcome.

> But he was angry and refused to go in. His father came out and entreated him, but he answered his father, "Look, these many years I have served you, and I never disobeyed your command, yet you never gave me a young goat, that I might celebrate with my friends. But when this son of yours came, who has devoured your property with prostitutes, you killed the fattened calf for him!" (Luke 15: 28–30)

Anger, disdain, self-righteousness, shaming, comparison, and bitterness marked his response. He wanted no part of the father's honor if he didn't get credit for his own. He was not rejoicing in obedience because his obedience had been motivated out of self-righteousness and self-protection. He believed he deserved to be rewarded in accordance with his outward *goodness* ("these many years I have served you, and I never disobeyed your command")—I mean, he would've fit right in with my Chinese upbringing! Think about it: the older brother kept *mianzi* and never caused his father to *diu lian*; he was successful at outrunning any form of shame. No broken pots at the city gates for him!

But he missed God's grace. He missed God's blessing. He missed the fullness of his father's table on account of his own self-striving.

Tim Keller said this about the older brother:

> It is not his sins that are keeping him from sharing in the feast of the father so much as his "righteousness." The elder brother in the end is lost, not despite his good record, but because of

Herein lies the
whole *reason*
we must
cease striving
through good works :
they do *not save*.

it. Now we are getting to the heart of how the gospel differs from the moral grid. As one writer put it, "The main thing between you and God is not your sins, but your damnable good works."[6]

Ouch. And herein lies the whole reason we must cease striving through good works: they do not save.

If there is a gospel of self-improvement, it is a damning one. It is a gospel that is not good news at all; it will wall you off, shrivel you up, and destroy your sensitivity to God's pursuit. This is why it must be utterly destroyed and replaced with the true gospel of life-transforming grace. Only the grace of God is enough to bring us home, make us worthy, and keep us in the love of God.

EIGHT

The Gift

Striving to Have It All

The man who has God for his treasure has all things in one.

—A. W. TOZER

'm not sure when I realized the American dream wasn't all that it was made out to be. Don't misunderstand—I still believe in America, its ideals, and the astounding privileges we get to experience as citizens of this country. I'm talking about the unicorn version of the American dream—the one that's always looking for bigger, better, more extravagant, greater comfort.

The idea of the American dream has blinded more than a few women in the quest for more. But maybe even more so, it's caused women like you and me to chase after the ever-before-us You Can

Have It All carrot. Some, in this day and age, say it out loud—speaking their declared goals of private jets, status, or marks of success over themselves.

The rest of us don't say it aloud, but we act as if it's attainable with a little more maneuvering or hustle. In most of our minds, the dream generally looks something like this:

- a romantic husband
- a clean home
- obedient children
- loyal communities
- a secure career
- clean eating
- a consistent workout schedule
- a thriving church that welcomes our gifts
- a balanced life
- friendly neighbors
- a trained family dog
- a clean refrigerator
- being debt-free in ten years
- parents who know just when and how much to weigh in on your life
- a well-kept lawn
- vacations that don't wear you out
- trustworthy girlfriends
- pillows that stay on the couch

You know, nothing *too* crazy or outlandish. Reasonable asks, right? As long as we do what we need to do to ensure it all comes to pass.

And then, other times, our lists of demands are hidden in a posture of Hard to Please. When others go with the flow, Hard to Please finds what's not up to par. She's quick to point out the missed opportunity and the better option. She's too overwhelmed with analyzing what could have been to enjoy what *actually is*, right now. Hard to Please is too busy trying to hold everything together to notice the eggshell path she's allowed to form between her and the people she cares about.

I was raised by a mother who had years of hurts and trauma to work through, many of which I still don't fully understand. As a result, she often acted out her pain when I was a child. Some of the dysfunctional aspects of our relationship seemed normal when I was too young to know the difference, but with time, I started noticing how much the lens through which I saw myself, the world, the relationships around me, and ultimately God, were deeply impacted by the unrest and striving that marked her own worldview prior to truly coming to rest in Christ. I have stories—maybe not the same, but similarly impacting—like the stories that have shaped you. Maybe your stories involve your mother or maybe someone equally influential.

God chose to draw me to himself by writing into my story a confusing tension between two cultures, a painful "unspoken broken" (as my dear friend Ann says) in my childhood home, and a journey to the Lord that involved a whole lot of unlearning of self-preserving cultural norms and replacing them with the self-surrendering gospel of grace.

My mom and I are more alike than we are different, even with all the hurts, history, and heartbreaks. Like most daughters, I had a list of things I wanted to emulate of my mother, and some things I didn't. And as it is with many daughters, the things we don't care to emulate are typically woven into the fabric of what is both nature and nurture—a twisted knot of who we are and who we're expected to be.

As a young wife and mother myself, I swore I'd never adopt the self-centered sensitivities my mother exhibited in a particular area of identity and worth: gift giving and receiving. I vowed I wouldn't be the type of woman who was Hard to Please. A wife and mother who criticized a less-than-spectacular Mother's Day gift, expected her husband to read her mind, lost it over a forgotten holiday, or pouted over a gift that signaled her apparent lack of worth—all because of her own standards and measurement of significance. I vowed to break with the example I'd been given.

Until I found myself doing the same things.

Maybe I didn't repeat the same actions over the same circumstances, but I was certainly driven by the same fears, the same expectations, the same feelings of being seen as not enough and then stubbornly being Hard to Please.

I didn't want to see it, but it was clear to me (and to Troy and the boys) that my discontent was more than nature, more than nurture, and more than environment (even if all these were contributions). Having a mother who wrestled with deep-seated insecurities, trauma, and pain only revealed my own natural need for approval. I saw it in her and sometimes resented her for it, but the truth was and is that she didn't teach me something that wasn't already there in myself. My mother's weaknesses only revealed how much we are more alike than we are different.

I'm embarrassed to admit how many silly tears I've shed over less-than-ideal gifts I misjudged as careless, and how many *not-so-silly* tears I've shed while on the receiving end of my mother's misjudging. It might have looked like pride (and in some ways, it was) for either of us to be demanding and critical, but behind every unmet standard of perfection or ideal was a striving to satisfy the unrelenting master of self-worship that promises you will be enough if you, and everyone else around you, will *just try harder.*

Like Hard to Please, Try Harder is the regime of an Enemy that knows we will be deceived into thinking we can manage or control our circumstances in order to gain what was meant to be only attainable through God's provision. Whether it's the persistent desire for another to meet our standards or the restlessness you struggle with until you meet those standards yourself, Try Harder makes a god of our expectations. It dangles personal and circumstantial perfection out there like a mirage—so within reach yet morphing into something else, something that never satisfies. Our Enemy knows he can fool us. When we are ruled by the Try Harder regime, we think we are getting closer to our perception of God when we're really just getting ever closer to the worship of self.

Why can't others do things my way?

I will make myself happy since no one else will.

My feelings come first.

I wouldn't have these issues if others would just choose to do better.

If these thoughts have ever lingered in your mind, you, too, may have unknowingly subscribed to a false theology of satisfaction via self-improvement (or others-improvement). You may be worshiping the Try Harder gospel. The gospel according to Jesus—the gospel of grace—eradicates the notion that any person has the ability to conquer emptiness with striving to please or to be pleased. The gospel is God's gift of true satisfaction. How, you might be asking?

- *God satisfies with his Word.* "I am the bread of life; whoever comes to me shall not hunger, and whoever believes in me shall never thirst" (John 6:35).
- *God satisfies with his presence.* "In your presence there is fullness of joy; at your right hand are pleasures forevermore" (Ps. 16:11).
- *God satisfies with his rule over everything.* "Cease striving and know that I am God; I will be exalted among the nations, I will be exalted in the earth" (Ps. 46:10 NASB).

I regularly find comfort in the words penned through the psalmist just above—so much so that they informed the titling of this book. They may be familiar to you as well. We often quote this Psalm and these verses to instill peace, reciting them in soft and hushed tones of assurance. Some might imagine a bluebird sitting contentedly on a blooming branch. Serene and at rest. (And, ahem, some of us have painted and reproduced these words as watercolor prints sold on the internet.) But the context of this Psalm is anything but fluffy and self-affirming. The context is war and distress.

> *God is our refuge and strength,*
> *A very present help in trouble.*
> *Therefore we will not fear, though the earth should change*
> *And though the mountains slip into the heart of the sea;*
> *Though its waters roar and foam,*
> *Though the mountains quake at its swelling pride.*
> *Selah.*
> *There is a river whose streams make glad the city of God,*

The holy dwelling places of the Most High.
God is in the midst of her, she will not be moved;
God will help her when morning dawns.
The nations made an uproar, the kingdoms tottered;
He raised His voice, the earth melted.
The LORD of hosts is with us;
The God of Jacob is our stronghold.
Selah.
Come, behold the works of the LORD,
Who has wrought desolations in the earth.
He makes wars to cease to the end of the earth;
He breaks the bow and cuts the spear in two;
He burns the chariots with fire.
"Cease striving and know that I am God;
I will be exalted among the nations,
I will be exalted in the earth."
The LORD of hosts is with us;
The God of Jacob is our stronghold.
Selah. (Psalm 46)

The psalmist wrote a song contrasting the turmoil of our lives with God's mighty power and infinitely greater strength. He described our worst fears, even now in our modern-day context: the crumbling of foundations, raging storms, falling kingdoms, war and violence. But the closing of this Psalm ends with words from God himself, and they aren't warm and fuzzy; they're more of a command. The original Hebrew word used here means to relax, release, to let go of your death grip, to stop wringing your hands in anxious worry.

It's as if God interjected in the midst of all our turmoil and chaos and declared, "Enough already. I'm enough, and you are not. So stop trying to fix everything and rest in me."

Such irony to think that the sense of rest and fulfillment he was talking about is exactly what we're trying to achieve in all of our busyness. So often we're blind to the fact that God is offering this rest to us now. Instead, we insist on reaching for it ourselves and, in so doing, fall into idolatry, the heart of which is the worship of something other than God—*lesser than God*. Idolatry is treasuring something or someone so much you're willing to do things your way instead of God's to possess it. The things we idolize can be tangible, yes, like money and jobs and friends and food, but more often than not, idolatry involves bowing down to my *ideas and expectations* for comfort and happiness in my life. It's wanting to have everything I want on my terms, by my own means.

And when it comes to God, idolatry is the belief that we can wield our worship to get what we want. When we apply that to God, we act out of a belief that God is someone we appease through striving. We can call it spiritual discipline, hard work, commitment, or pursuit of holiness, but if it's motivated by self-fulfillment or self-improvement, it's not a worship of God; it's a worship of self. Typically, if we obsess over organization and well-kept schedules, we don't call it false worship; we call that being super organized. But, truth is, whether we are going through the motions, inauthentically worshiping a God we don't actually know by heart, or whether we're chasing after false gods like routine or schedules, both are false worship when the end goal of our efforts is to get what we think will get us further, rather than to get more of God.

What if our striving is really worship of ourselves *as* god? If this is true, we stand to miss the gift of grace—the gift of rest and satisfaction.

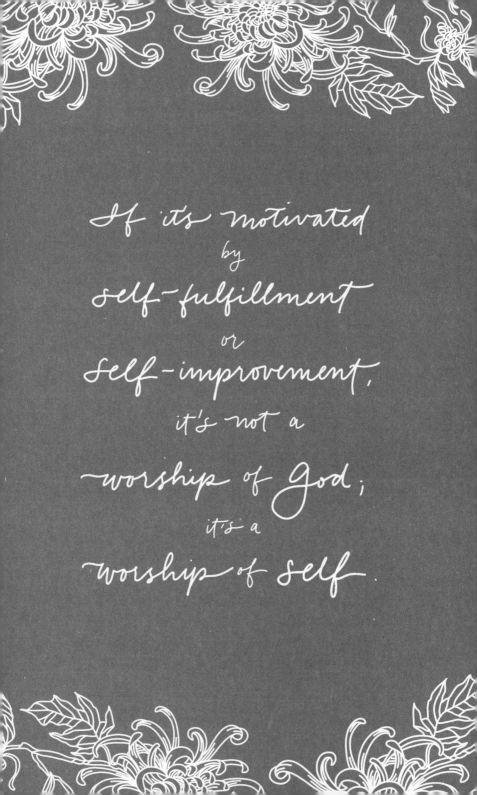

If it's motivated by self-fulfillment or self-improvement, it's not a worship of God; it's a worship of self.

Does any of this remind you of a time when God promised rest and satisfaction to his children? Does it make you think of the promised land, offered to the Israelites but inaccessible because they didn't trust God? Rest and satisfaction are essentially what awaited the Israelites in the promised land. Rest from their toils and striving, satisfaction for their hunger and longings. And you may remember, they couldn't access God's promised rest in their disbelief, fear, and distrust. They couldn't receive the land even when they tried to take it with their own hands with fervor (Deut. 1:41–42). An entire generation minus two missed out on God's promised gift as a result of trusting themselves more than God. The Israelites did not settle the Land of Milk and Honey until they believed and trusted the God who promised it.

Can you imagine being offered everything that brings rest and fulfillment but choosing doubt and self-sufficiency instead? Unthinkable, right? Except that's exactly what I so often see in my own life. Believing my own way in and through the wilderness is somehow more effective than God's way—this is the perpetual false worship in my life, and the promised land of "having it all" is the idol. Until the Israelites listened, obeyed, and trusted God for his provision his way, they missed out on his gift of rest and satisfaction. God wasn't micromanaging how his children received his gifts; he was preparing them to understand that the promised land was just the beginning, but none of what was to come could ever be accessed through self-striving. He was after their hearts.

As someone raised along the fringes of the East-Asian mindset, I read the account of the Israelites' forty years in the wilderness, unable to receive the gift of God's ultimate provision in the promised land, and can't help but wonder how these "children" couldn't figure it out, perform up to God's standards, and receive their gift. But for God, this was not an exchange of performance and meeting expectation. This was an exercise to instill humility and surrender in a people who resisted the audacious provisions of a God who performed impossible works of wonder to rescue his kids and bring them out of slavery. Maybe, like the Israelites, we are so wired to doubt anything we've not earned that we miss the ticket of admission into God's promises: the gift of grace. Maybe we can't believe we were made to receive gifts we don't deserve, and maybe we have lingering stories that keep us from seeing the truth of God's countercultural ways. I know I do.

The Red Envelope

A long red envelope—subtle enough for a hundred-dollar bill to feel extravagant, but extravagant enough for even a single dollar bill to feel elevated. If you've ever received one, you know. It's a thing of elegance and expectation. The red envelope's edges are crisp and, if adorned, exquisite. The flap is sealed, and until the moment it's delivered to the recipient, the *hongbao* is kept carefully and pristinely tucked away.

Like all Chinese children, I learned to anticipate the *hongbao*. But there are rules:

- Red envelopes are given at Chinese New Year, weddings, or special celebrations and are only given by someone older and in authority.
- Only crisp, new bills, no crinkly money or coins from your wallet, may go in the envelope.

- Envelopes must be red for good luck.
- Oh—and don't give bills in quantities that include the number four because *four* in Mandarin sounds like the word for "death." And death is unlucky.
- And no odd numbers, just even please. Because odd numbers are unlucky.

And there's etiquette:

- Never open a *hongbao* in front of the presenter.
- Decline the gift at first before receiving it.
- Receive it with both hands, and children should bow.
- And if it's the Lunar New Year, don't forget to say, *"Gong xi fa cai."*

I found the tradition fascinating, but I didn't love the way I felt in the exchange—an exchange that isn't unique to the red envelope but that anyone at any Christmas morning, birthday dinner, or graduation party might experience. You may even experience it virtually when given a shout-out on social media. It's the tension between worthiness and unworthiness. Gratitude and guilt. Met or unmet expectations. It's the tension of wondering where affection ends and obligation begins.

Formalities and rules don't ensure love, assurance, or gratitude (and I think love, assurance, or gratitude are what we are looking for in giving and receiving gifts); they simply facilitate expectations and how to meet them.

Like a red envelope that silently signals an orchestrated dance of honor and respect, expectations and qualification, I wonder if we are sometimes tempted to view the gift of grace—from

God—as a ritual of forced etiquette within an unspoken exchange that determines and secures worthiness.

Ritual can feel reverent, but without relationship, assurance is fleeting and love is questionable.

Have we mistakenly imposed a set of rules for receiving the gift of God, hoping to contain all that is infinitely mysterious and impossibly difficult about fully grasping redeeming grace—the ultimate gift of God?

And then we wonder, after following all the tidy rules and self-made standards: *Is this as good as it gets?*

I'm here to tell you no—it's not.

Here's what I know about God's gift of grace:

- *We didn't deserve it and did nothing to merit his favor toward us.* "But God, being rich in mercy, because of the great love with which he loved us, even when we were dead in our trespasses, made us alive together with Christ" (Eph. 2:4–5).
- *God pursued us with love and intention to pull us out of the sinkhole of misery and self-sufficiency, and he made us fit to be with Jesus through Jesus.* "By grace you have been saved—and raised us up with him and seated us with him in the heavenly places in Christ Jesus, so that in the coming ages he might show the immeasurable riches of his grace in kindness toward us in Christ Jesus" (vv. 5–7).
- *He made it abundantly clear that it was his idea, his provision, his way, and his gift.* "For by grace you have been saved through faith. And this is not your own doing; it is the gift of God, not a result of works, so that no one may boast" (vv. 8–9).

a *gift* with an invoice due upon receipt is **No** gift at all.

God eliminates the tension of his gift by pronouncing us as unworthy to begin with and by declaring, with tremendous clarity, that his rescue was motivated by mercy and love. We don't have to question his motivation. God's only obligation was to his own holiness; his love for us did not have to end for his obligation to justice to begin. Both were met in the cross of Christ.

What if we didn't skip over this passage from Ephesians 2 but sat with it, thought on it, let it sweep over us with truth that we didn't dismiss as impractical doctrine? Friend, I wonder if this is why some of us keep limping along in our walks with God, struggling to know where we stand. Is this why so many of us struggle to feel freedom rather than obligation in our relationships with God? Why some still think to be a Christ follower is to follow rules?

For so long I looked at the gift of God like the gift that came with rules and etiquette. Him, bearing down with his authority, requiring proper etiquette and a perfect two-handed, bowing reception. Me, wondering if God really loved me or if this gift was but an obligation or a display of his expectations for my good behavior. It was all rather me-centered. And it turns out, a me-centered view of anything, including one's theology, is the lens through which we end up seeing the skewed ideas of never enough and forever needing self-improvement.

All I ever really wanted—what anyone really wants—is to be worthy of a gift that comes with no strings attached. After all, a gift with an invoice due upon receipt is no gift at all.

PART 2

When Grace Changes Everything

NINE

Grace Makes New, Not Better

Therefore, if anyone is in Christ, he is a new creation. The old has passed away; behold, the new has come.

—2 CORINTHIANS 5:17

y hope is that, by now, I have sufficiently convinced you that striving for self-improvement is a dead-end street.

The temptation to fix yourself, better yourself, feel good about yourself by cleaning yourself up—that temptation is real. And as we've seen thus far, we aren't alone in this; there's a long line of religious folks and self-help gurus selling the power of hard work and achievement. And truth is, hard work and achievement are commendable, but they lack power as sources for true change.

My goal has been to show you that striving in our own strength to attain any form of worth, approval, assurance, or comfort will never deliver on the promises it makes. But now that we agree—regardless of how similar or different our stories look—that we are by nature strivers and self-improvers, I want to show you this: that self-righteous striving is more hopeless than you want to believe, but grace is more life-transforming than you realize. There isn't merely good news for our bad news; there's a way forward and a way out of the cycle of anxious hustling, self-condemnation, and proving ourselves.

Here's where I want to draw out our coffee date and ask you to stay awhile. Right here is where I believe so many well-meaning Christian women get stuck and feel powerless along the way to understanding the gift of grace. Too many of us hear the hard truth that we aren't enough and don't know what to do in response.

Do we, then, sit idly by and wait for the Lord to do whatever he will in his sovereignty?

Do we just read our Bibles and hope change will magically come about?

Do we give up on the idea of improvement altogether and accept our sinful patterns and habits?

Do we keep hustling anxiously but pray that we will do it with God's strength?

Where does striving end and trusting begin?

I have asked all of these questions and, at times, defaulted to believing wrongly that the gospel is powerful enough to save me from hell but not powerful enough to save me *to* something greater than self-improvement.

I'm guessing you relate to one of the following:

· You've been worn out trying to be a better version of yourself.
· You've felt guilt or pressure about doing more, being more, accomplishing more.
· You've struggled to understand the place for good works if grace saves us.
· You're tired of trying to measure up to other people's standards.
· You can't decide if God is pleased with you or disappointed in you.
· You want to grow and change but don't know how it really happens.

I just want to voice these things out loud because I see you. I'm with you. And, listen, sometimes I wish *change* and *becoming* were a quick and easy formula too. Sometimes it's easier to subscribe to a twelve-step program than to submit to a lifelong process known as sanctification. But God promises us:

> I will give you a new heart, and a new spirit I will put within you. And I will remove the heart of stone from your flesh and give you a heart of flesh. And I will put my Spirit within you, and cause you to walk in my statutes and be careful to obey my rules. You shall dwell in the land that I gave to your fathers, and you shall be my people, and I will be your God. (Ezek. 36:26–28)

The prophet Ezekiel voiced these words from God that wouldn't be fully realized until the arrival of Christ, the Savior, but sometimes I wish our spiritual transformation truly happened like a heart transplant.

Some of you reading these pages may remember when our family walked the unknowns alongside Troy's younger brother who needed a new heart. His had failed, and he was placed on the top of a heart transplant list. I'll never forget receiving word that he had been matched and was due to go into surgery within the next day. Another family's deep and painful loss made life possible for my brother-in-law.

Troy and I flew out to meet with the rest of the family and the doctors who would operate on his brother. The whole family was called into a stark hospital meeting room to hear from the surgeon after the lengthy, mind-blowing procedure. (I still cannot wrap my mind around it!) We watched as the doctor drew diagrams and labeled ventricles. We listened and held our breaths as he described what they removed and what they placed in an empty cavity in my brother-in-law's chest. His broken heart was literally removed, and a new and healthy one was put in its place.

And it was now beating. It was pumping his blood. It was giving him new life.

It's no surprise that, as an artist, this visual is stunning, if not arresting, for me. How clear does God have to be about our utter need for new, not better—self-replacement, not self-betterment. The heart represents the center of a person's soul, the control center of one's desires, motives, spiritual being. God isn't in the business of replacing qualities, giftings, and perspectives unique to you; he's all about the lifesaving eviction of a diseased control center and replacing it with one that can make you operate and fulfill the purposes for which he created you.

That's why the gospel isn't a recipe for self-improvement. It's not a mix of working with what you've got, sprinkling in a little religious effort, adding in discipline, strategy, and a healthy dash of likability. But this formula (as we've seen in previous chapters) isn't entirely a recipe for disaster—if it were, we'd all have jumped ship like it was a bad fad diet we realized we'd taken up in a moment of weakness watching late-night television. No, unfortunately, this recipe sometimes yields results. It sometimes rewards those who keep on pushing, keep on hustling, keep on perfecting, keep on striving. But the fruit isn't lasting because the control center that's keeping us keeping on in this way was broken to begin with. It'll only run for so long in its terminal condition.

So, it's worth revisiting this key passage of Scripture that resets our operating system. I want you to know how important it is that you not miss what I'm about to say. *This* is what changes everything:

> But God, being rich in mercy, because of the great love with which he loved us, even when we were dead in our trespasses, made us alive together with Christ—by grace you have been saved—and raised us up with him and seated us with him in the heavenly places in Christ Jesus, so that in the coming ages he might show the immeasurable riches of his grace in kindness toward us in Christ Jesus. For by grace you have been saved through faith. And this is not your own doing; it is the gift of God, not a result of works, so that no one may boast. For we are his workmanship, created in Christ Jesus for good works, which God prepared beforehand, that we should walk in them. (Eph. 2:4–10)

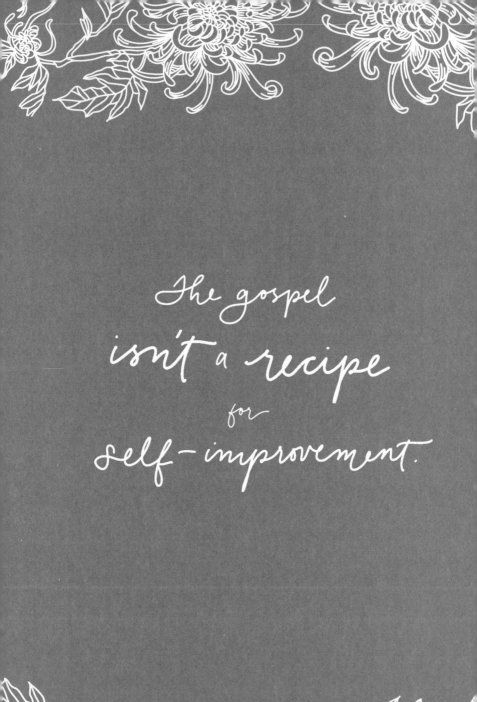

The gospel
isn't a recipe
for
self-improvement.

This passage begins with two little words that become the hinge of history—the moment where all the impossible becomes possible in our longing to be enough:

But God.

In the same way that all that comes before Ephesians 2:4 declares our alienation from God, the first half of this book is about our inability to save ourselves. But in steps God. Paul didn't tell us here in Ephesians that God fixes everything, makes us feel better, or gets rid of our deficiencies. In fact, Paul didn't say much about us at all. Instead, he made sure we would know all about God . . .

- who is rich in mercy,
- who greatly loves us,
- who intercepted our waywardness,
- and made us alive with Christ,
- who raised us up,
- and shows us the immeasurable riches of his grace and kindness,
- who saves us by his grace,
- molds us,
- and makes us first to do good works.

If there's one passage of Scripture that fully summarizes the benefits of grace, it's this one. Paul succinctly declared all that is fundamentally changed because of the grace of God. The words *but God* are our reminder that we can't, but God can.

For all of history, man was unable to meet God's standards, face the true consequences of sin, or answer for his lack of holiness before a righteous God. We were all found utterly and completely *not enough*. That nagging feeling we've had all along—that feeling of imperfection, ineptitude, or insufficiency? The world offers endless ways to stuff it down, cover it up, numb it out, compensate, and overcome our inadequacy, but Jesus offered—and still offers—the only true solution that wasn't temporary but eternal.

No sacrifice could solve the problem.

No amount of right living could make us whole.

No religious effort was enough to save a sinful heart.

Both the messy and broken, the pious and pretty, were equally incapable of loving the Lord with all their hearts, minds, souls, and strength. The most foundational command to love God above all else was broken in the garden; how could we possibly fix ourselves and make ourselves fit for God's approval if we aren't even able to love God wholly as we were made to do?

You see, the gospel is the good news because the bad news is without hope. And I can't help but wonder: If we really considered how bad the bad news is, and how good the good news of Jesus is, would we still feel as hopeless as we tend to feel when change doesn't happen fast, easily, or in the way we expect? Would we turn to self-help and self-improvement if we fell wholly on God's promise to sanctify us through grace?

The Bad News: Dead Means Dead

I'm not sure anyone but a Christ follower can find the silver lining in being called dead in our trespasses (Eph. 2:1). There's no good spin on such an indictment. Paul didn't mince words in Ephesians 2. He was to the point and clear as day: salvation is not about you or me. We were dead, made alive. Dead people can't do anything, so don't try to take credit for saving yourself.

"Dead in our trespasses" isn't a nice way to say that we are somewhat effective and overall okay with God. No, to be dead in trespasses is to be like the "ungrateful dead, spiritual zombies, death-walkers, unable even to understand the gravity of their situation. . . . They may go through the motions of life, but they do not possess it."[1] Dead means dead, and it isn't pretty. We won't find it on a hand-lettered plaque, and we don't share it on social media: *I was a spiritual zombie before I met Jesus!*

I know; this coffee date just got real heavy.

But that's really what Paul was describing here and why *but God* is our turning point. Grace isn't just the field of wildflowers you get to run through because you've been forgiven. Grace is the kindness of God that led you to that glorious field in the first place. Without grace, we wouldn't even know how desperately we are in need of it.

Matt Chandler said it succinctly this way: "Without a heart transformed by the grace of Christ, we just continue to manage external and internal darkness."[2]

When a flower dies, there's no reviving it. You can't dunk a cut, dried rose into a bucket of water and find its petals supple and still in bloom. You can only manage it in its dead state. You can preserve it in a dried floral arrangement or use its petals in potpourri (remember those sachets?), but you can't make a cut rose behave like a living bud on a rose bush. Sooner or later it will show itself to be, well, dead. So here's the gut-punching truth: if you are constantly trying to control outcomes, circumstances, and others' perception of you, you may be forfeiting the life-transforming power of redeeming grace. If management is to control things, people, or circumstances, then our efforts to manage the broken and insufficient in our lives will only result in the anxious maneuvering and manipulation of trying to preserve our own lives.

Made Alive: By Grace

So, how do the dead change and become alive? Paul clearly told us that God—out of love and mercy toward us—made it happen, by grace. Again: "But God, being rich in mercy, because of the great love with which he loved us, even when we were dead in our trespasses, made us alive together with Christ—by grace you have been saved" (vv. 4–5).

Here it is again, without all the parentheticals: "God . . . made us alive together with Christ."

He did it. God is the subject who carries out the action. He is the author of the grace by which we are saved.

I don't know about you, but I can start thinking about grace in some nebulous, nondescript way—taking the grit out of God's plan to rescue and reach us by the means of grace. When I started my personal blog in 2007 and called it *GraceLaced*, I thought I was being so conceptually fresh and clever. The word *grace* wasn't so ubiquitously added on to everything from pretty homes to happy thoughts—it carried weight, at least for me. And that smooshing of two words together? Well, I was really into that in the early 2000s. (So much so that I gave all the Simons boys middle names that compounded a word with *Li*, meaning *power* or *strength* in Chinese.) *GraceLaced*'s tagline was "finding grace in the everyday." My goal was simple. I wanted to discover how the grace of God intersected with—or laced itself through—my everyday, mundane, life. That's it. That's how GraceLaced was born, and later became a business, a lifestyle brand, and the name of my first book.

But what does *grace* really mean, and how do we recognize its benefits at work in our unexciting, everyday lives?

Grace is, by biblical definition, God's unmerited favor. In the New Testament, grace is derived from the Greek word *charis*, which carries the meaning of good will, loving-kindness, divine favor. But I think that definition falls a smidge short in light of all that the grace of God grants us and enables us to do. Though fully true and without error, this simple definition of grace alone keeps me from deeply appreciating and depending on grace as a life raft rather than a cruise ship. It may lead us to see God's favor as but the cherry on top of our places to go and people to see, unless we recognize that we are stuck—dead, lifeless, helplessly treading water—if not for deliverance through the grace of God.

While we were completely, helplessly dead, God made the impossible possible by the work of merciful grace. Now let's wrap our minds around how we access this grace.

Access: Through Faith

"For by grace you have been saved through faith. And this is not your own doing; it is the gift of God, not a result of works, so that no one may boast" (vv. 8–9).

Through—moving or transferring from one location to another via a channel or corridor. From one state of being to another. If we are dead in our sin and made alive by God, then faith is the key that unlocks the gift of grace that makes this transformation possible. As in, the gift is just there—available and waiting. But it is faith that allows us to take hold of it. The same Paul that penned these words in Ephesians 2 explained this access in Romans 5: "Through him [Jesus] we have also obtained access by faith into this grace in which we stand, and we rejoice in hope of the glory of God" (v. 2).

Though still insufficient as an illustration, I picture this access as akin to receiving an invitation to dinner at the White House. You can't get in unless you've been granted an invitation. You must access that invitation by receiving it, opening it, RSVPing for it. But once you accept the invitation and show up for dinner, you don't need to continually flash your invitation; you've gained access, and your place is secure. You *stand* in the promise of that gift, that welcome. Even if the analogy falls short, it serves at some level to remind us that God hosts the banquet, God is the initiator, God offers an invitation without cost to his guests. All they must do is receive his invitation and enter. By grace through faith.

If grace is activated in us through faith, then it's important to know how we exercise faith. The writer of Hebrews told us, "Now faith is the assurance of things hoped for, the conviction of things not seen" (Heb. 11:1). I love what Bible scholars say about the Greek word from which we get "assurance" in this verse. It's the word *hupostasis*, which is formed from the word *stasis*, "to stand" and *hupo*, "under," together conveying the sense that faith is the evidence of ownership—or "title deed"—of what can't be seen. In other words, faith is standing secure like one who holds the deed to a treasure that can't be taken away. Here's how another version puts it:

> Now faith is the assurance (title deed, confirmation) of things
> hoped for (divinely guaranteed), and the evidence of things

not seen [the conviction of their reality—faith comprehends as fact what cannot be experienced by the physical senses]. (AMP)

I like this definition: "Faith transports God's promises into the present tense. . . . Real faith implicitly takes God at His word. Faith is a supernatural confidence in—and therefore reliance on—the One who has made the promises."[3]

This means that faith is placed *on* something or someone; it's not just a feeling or vague sense of hopefulness. When Jesus is our guarantor, when he is the one who keeps his promises, we have a firm foundation on which to place our assurance. We access grace *through faith* by believing what God says and actively trusting in it. *By grace through faith* is how we can really, truly *cease striving* and know that he is God.

Purpose: Created for Good Works

"For we are his workmanship, created in Christ Jesus for good works, which God prepared beforehand, that we should walk in them" (Eph. 2: 10).

Paul didn't end this section in the second chapter of Ephesians without giving us the purpose for this transformation from spiritual death to life. Unlike a cut flower that fades and can't be changed but only preserved with the right conditions, a bud on a tree will bloom and makes way for fruit. Living blooms produce living fruit.

In many ways, this book is for doers—for those of us who want to get busy and accomplish things, check things off our lists, and make something of ourselves because in so doing we hope to find peace, rest, comfort, or a sense of purpose. For us doers, doing equals progress—even spiritual responsibility, perhaps. We think, even if subconsciously, that not being a doer, living solely on the concept of grace, means being a lazy dreamer, abdicating our roles, actively choosing not to bear fruit. But that couldn't be further from the truth. The gospel of life-transforming grace isn't the opposite of exhibiting good fruit; it's the fuel that allows us to do so.

That's why Paul didn't end this passage in Ephesians about being given the gift of grace with, "So now you're okay, you're accepted, you're done with striving! Go enjoy your life!" He bookended the gift of grace with God's love and mercy and our fruitfulness in response to him.

This is where we are headed in the next several chapters. I'm not out to convince you that grace is enough to save you just as you are presently so that you can stay the same. In fact, anything less than genuine progress toward real change is an outworking of cheap grace. What do I mean by that? I'll let Dietrich Bonhoeffer define it succinctly:

> Cheap grace means . . . [g]race without price; grace without cost! The essence of grace, we suppose, is that the account has been paid in advance; and, because it has been paid, everything can be had for nothing. Since the cost was infinite, the possibilities of using and spending it are infinite . . . Cheap grace is grace without discipleship, grace without the cross, grace without Jesus Christ, living and incarnate . . . [Costly] grace is *costly* because it calls us to follow, and it is *grace* because it calls us to follow Jesus Christ. It is costly

because it costs a man his life, and it is grace because it gives a man the only true life.[4]

The only true life. How much is that worth? Everything—our holiness, forgiveness of others, our turning from the idols of fear and control, self and striving.

You see, it's not enough to see our striving as worthless; we must see God's grace as most valuable and costly. My goal for the remainder of our time together is to show you how stunning God's grace really is, and that the amazing grace of God is the power by which we are rescued from ourselves and thus transformed in newness of life. Only then will we see the fruit of change we long for. This is where we're headed these next several chapters—to understand and grasp this amazing means of life transformation called *grace.*

I spent too many years thinking God saved me so that I could get my act together and be a better version of myself; I didn't fully understand the gospel. That's not the grace of God. I wasted so much time hoping more consistency, better choices, swearing off persistent sin, or hiding from God would help me feel more worthy. But no more. We can declare *no more* to the almost-gospel-but-not-quite versions of redemption. No more salvation via support groups alone. No more peace through perpetual perfection. No more gauging our enoughness by popular opinion.

We who were once dead are now made alive. Grace is not a betterment plan; it's a total replacement offer.

Paul, in 2 Corinthians, told us, "Therefore, if anyone is in

Grace
is not a
betterment plan;
it's a **total**
replacement offer.

Christ, he is a new creation. The old has passed away; behold, the new has come" (5:17).

And lest you think this a mere rallying cry with pom-poms and confetti, I'll let you in on where we're going. We're not going to be satisfied with a quick pep talk or a relatable story or two if we are to cease earthly striving for the remainder of our life journeys. We are going to need much more than that. I'm going to show you how to persevere, remain, and continue to strive . . . but strive in grace, by grace, and through grace alone.

I like how Jerry Bridges put it: "Your worst days are never so bad that you are beyond the *reach* of God's grace. And your best days are never so good that you are beyond the *need* of God's grace."[5]

We will never find ourselves needing grace any less. We will only recognize how great our desperation and how much more sufficient the grace of God is to meet that need. And, it turns out, grace—which replaces all the favor we strive to attain for ourselves—is truly enough to make you and me more than our grandest views of *better* and instead make us brand new.

TEN

Grace Fuels Good Works

God is able to make all grace abound to you,
so that having all sufficiency in all things at all
times, you may abound in every good work.
—2 Corinthians 9:8 ESV

he Chinese American church in which my parents came to faith was likely much like yours: beautiful, messy, and imperfect. Any body of believers is made up of the sinful, sick, dysfunctional, and hurting—all of us who realize we're hopeless apart from the grace of God. Ours just happened to sing songs in Mandarin and followed every service with a potluck of epic proportions that always included Auntie Liu's famous *chow fun* and our Malaysian-born pastor's fish head stew. Get yourself to an Asian church service, friends, and stay afterward. You won't be sorry.

What makes the church beautiful is that it is diverse and not monolithic in the way believers worship, the instruments they use, or the way they incorporate their heritages or cultural contexts. But at times, we can let cultural norms and values influence the gospel in a way that causes us to believe that Jesus plus *something else* saves us. I think one of the reasons why I've had a complicated battle with striving and performance is, in part, due to the fact that Asian culture is itself prone to legalism.

If legalism, as we understand it in the Bible, is an adherence to rules and moral goodness as a way to appease God, it's similar in its focus to the idol worship found in many Asian cultures. The goal in these religions is to appease a god through the right set of actions. Good actions lead to (hopefully) a desired response from the god you worship. Cause and effect. Burn the incense, bring the offering, follow the rules.

When I was in my tween years—when my parents were young believers, doing the best they knew how to lead their family in this newfound faith they didn't fully understand—my mother would offer what she thought was a helpful remedy to my problems. If I said, "I had such a hard day at school," her response would be, "Did you have your quiet time?" While it wouldn't be her response now, as a more mature believer, it was her default back then as someone new in the faith. Back then, it was her natural bent to think of God as a deity who grants favor when we've followed the rules or behaved properly, withholding favor when we don't. Doing or not doing my "devotions" seemed akin to bowing or not bowing correctly. My blessings depended on it. I grew to waffle back and forth between feeling confident in my well-kept "quiet times" and feeling condemned that I brought a hard day on myself when I missed one. Believing and acting this way leaves you fearful, unsure, always waiting for the other favor-shoe to drop. It's exhausting to try to avoid punishment with good behavior. That's where legalism leaves you.

Of course, years later, I now understand the benefit of spending time in the Word, whether I call it "devotions" or not. The magic isn't in the formula of a praise song, short reading, verse memory, and prayer. I don't secure a carefree or conflict-free day (or life) by clocking time in the Word. The goal, instead, is to know my savior more deeply through worship and the study of his love letter to me, his Word. But how do we move from obligation to delight, legalism to love? And if legalism is so bad and ineffective, why did God give us his law or his rules in the first place?

The Law Was Never Meant to Save

Though it marks the beginning of a believer's transformation as a new creation, the work of grace, in the sense that it was poured out on us through the crucifixion of Jesus, is the finish line mankind has long ached for. Jesus finally accomplished what human beings could not. That's what he meant when he said, "It is finished" (John 19:30). Jesus declared his work of redemption a finished work because before then, the people of God could not satisfy God's righteous and holy requirements simply through rule-following or adhering to the Law. They tried and tried. They made offerings, they made rules for the rules, and they continually sought to close the gap between God's holiness and their fallenness.

> Now before faith came, we were held captive under the law, imprisoned until the coming faith would be revealed. So then, the law was our guardian until Christ came, in order that we might be justified by faith. (Gal. 3:23–24)

Another version states verse 24 this way: "the law was our tutor to bring us to Christ" (NKJV).

In other words, God's righteous requirements of his people could never be met by their own efforts and only served to remind them how much they needed a savior. The Law drove them to understand their need for redeeming grace. Simply put—if you feel like God has impossible standards, you're right. The amazing grace of God is that he fulfilled his own standards on your behalf through the perfect finished work of Christ's life, death, burial, and resurrection. The efforts to restore a right relationship with God through rule-following and rituals were a futile and vain pursuit, leaving God's people worn out and unable to fulfill the Law's demands, so "Christ redeemed us from the curse of the law by becoming a curse for us" (v. 13). When we try to fulfill those standards once again with moral and right living, we choose the very legalism Christ came to destroy.

The result of Christ's redemptive work was that we would be made wholly fit for the Holy Spirit to dwell within us, enabling us to no longer work to try to gain access to the Father but to be children, trained and equipped to do as he instructs.

If you had told my college-aged self that I would one day be a mother to six boys—and love it—I would have called you crazy. I would have told you that I don't particularly like children, can't imagine ballooning out physically six times over the course of ten years, and that I'm the most unlikely person to mother well. If parenting requires patience, wisdom, discipline, discernment, a gentle tone of voice, *not* overreacting, organization, multitasking, biblical knowledge, a calm spirit, or consistency in training a child to obey day after day, I'm not the natural choice. In fact, I am, by nature, missing those particular skills and strengths.

Some of you highly favored sisters out there (God bless you) have an exceptionally nurturing touch, always seem to know how to soothe the angry toddler in the nursery, sing delightful songs to preschoolers, and willingly sign up to teach Vacation Bible School. Not me.

My six sons are a daily reminder to me that God does the impossible and changes hearts. They are more than I deserve, and I'm so proud to be their mama. But sometimes I think God gave me this gaggle of boys to keep me humble, to show me my weaknesses, and to illustrate in very tangible ways how God desires obedience and good works in the life of a believer.

As a mom, I'm constantly in pursuit of answers to questions like: How do I help these boys change? How do I teach them to think wisely, turn from wrong, and make right choices? If I'm honest, I want the transformation process to be swift, immediate, and a one-and-done. I'm pretty much an expert at barking out orders while demanding unquestioning compliance. (Anyone else?) At my worst, I can embody a kind of parenting that only looks to measurables—good works, good grades, good choices, good attitudes. A kind of parenting that rules *with rules*. Left to myself, I'd be naturally prone to seek results even at the expense of relationship. But God is just the opposite, which is why I apparently need these daily reminders of how much I need Jesus.

God doesn't demand obedience and good fruit apart from relationship. He desires our obedience as a result of relationship with him. He's after our hearts. Even all the way back in the garden, God gave his instructions to Adam and Eve within the intimacy of relationship. A choice to follow his instructions didn't earn them God's presence—they already walked with God—but their choice to disobey cost them their unhindered fellowship with him in the garden. That very separation is why Jesus had to restore what was lost, and the reason why we can once again obey in response to his favor rather than obey to achieve his favor. God's rules are always set within the context of his desire for us to know him and his heart for us as a good Father.

Strive in Grace

If you've spent any time in the epistles—letters written by disciples in the New Testament—you may have noticed a pattern. In conveying important instructions, exhortations, and reminders to the young churches learning to live out their faith as a community, these letters all began with clear reminders of biblical truth.

Sure, the reader would have already known the gospel, but Paul, for example, who wrote the letter to the Colossians, waited to instruct until after he realigned the reader with the truth of Christ and redemption. Why? Why was it so important for him to repeat himself, to restate what should have been obvious and already known?

Because we forget who we belong to, forget who our Father is, forget what he's done for us. Because we get out of alignment. Paul and the other writers of the epistles reminded us of all these things because it's easy to fall back into a pattern of striving *for* grace rather than striving *in* grace. The first chapters of these epistles remind believers of who they are in Christ, and they were written that way on purpose. These defining doctrinal chapters set the stage for the practical outworking later in the letters with instructions on what we then do in response to having been saved by grace through faith.

Take, for example, the instructions in Colossians 2:6–7: "Therefore, as you received Christ Jesus the Lord, so walk in him, rooted and built up in him and established in the faith, just as you were taught, abounding in thanksgiving."

If you look closely, there's an active verb in there. "So walk in him" is a direct command. Notice Paul didn't say, "Therefore relax." He told believers that, because their rescue from the law was so freeing, they could now strive to walk in the grace they'd received. We can strive in grace. I think we tend to imagine that receiving God's grace is to rock gently in a hammock with an iced tea in hand, with no care in the world. That's just not an accurate picture of a grace-filled life.

Don't you see? Grace is not the reward in itself; knowing Christ is. Grace simply makes it possible for you to stop striving for yourself and strive out of love for God instead. Grace isn't an excuse to be lazy or apathetic about the marks of a Christian life. Rather, it is the catalyst by which we can partake in it. Friend, we've not been saved by grace and spared the ceaselessness of

It's easy to fall back into a **pattern** of striving _for_ grace rather than striving _in_ grace.

striving so that we can stay the same. When we are informed by grace and not conformed to the law, we can strive the way we ought.

Now, let's look at what it means to live out the grace we've been given, and how we are to strive in grace.

Make Straight the Way of the Lord

Once we've been firmly grounded in the truth of who we are and how we've been saved, we move on to the practical outworking of those truths. When we consider all that underlies the gift of grace—the purchase of our freedom from the law—we realize how significant it is that Paul began Colossians 2:6 with "therefore," moving our attention from *positional*—as in "where do you stand with God?"—to *practical* truth, as in "so what then?" He was addressing how we respond to this finished work of Christ.

Paul said something similar just a bit further on in his letter, in Colossians 3:1, as he began practical instructions on how to walk as believers and alongside other believers. He used an if/then structure: "If then you have been raised with Christ, see the things that are above, where Christ is, seated at the right hand of God."

Both examples show us how Paul used the truth of what we know to determine how we should proceed. There's instruction to strive, to act; it's just not striving to gain a position with God—it is a striving that results from an already secure place with Jesus. Paul took us from *doctrine* to *doing*, from *why* to *how*.

A fancy word for right conduct or practice is the word *ortho-praxy* (*ortho* means straight, *praxy* is practice), or *commands*.

Orthopraxy is what we do because of our faith, and orthodoxy is what we believe. Orthodoxy tells us what is straight; orthopraxy tells us how to walk along that straight line. I know I'm getting word nerdy here for a minute, but I just want to make sure you see the point that orthopraxy is always fueled by true orthodoxy.

Orthodoxy can be such an unpopular word these days because it feels rigid, narrow, or unyielding, but I'll be honest: I'm team orthodoxy and long for more sound biblical thinking in this world of loose, wide, inclusive believing. You don't have to agree with me, and I'm not here to convince you to be on my team. I'm simply hoping to be a little lighthouse in the foggy mess of any-path-to-God and to shine the light on God's prescription for hope, transformation, and true satisfaction. It's by grace alone.

Orthodoxy is like light; orthopraxy is like heat. And we need both. This is what I mean:

I think the Enemy would have us sever the tie between the two—to be all love, passion, and action (all really important things!) without the anchor of truth, alignment, and the whole counsel of Scripture, or vice versa. Our Enemy would love for us to chase after one or the other because either, alone, lacks power. Neither, alone, can save, can sustain, or can impact true change. He knows that when we're most bent toward being laser-focused on doctrine and knowledge without love and action, our walk is cold—like an LED light that might illumine but can't provide warmth.

But when we overemphasize what we *do* for God—the justice, causes, or beautiful humanitarian services we fight for—apart from the truth of the gospel, our impassioned desire to effect change is all heat without light. Our efforts are like embers, which are cozy but can't light the path for the long haul.

Without the orthodoxy—or what is true about who God is and what he's done—the orthopraxy would be basically impossible. (Remember? Without the grace of God to rescue us, we'd still be dead. And it's impossible for the spiritually dead to please God.) Attempting to do great things *for* God without trusting in the great things he's already done for us will always lead to either a whole lot of self-righteousness or total despair and distance from God, fearing that you've failed him.

Cold orthodoxy—light without heat—was God's accusation of the church at Ephesus in the book of Revelation. But the early church also oftentimes embraced heat without light. It was a problem then, and it's a problem now. You see, without light or truth, what we *do* will be left up to opinion, culture, and what feels right. That's the day in which we live.

I'm convinced there's a reason we are so addicted to self-help resources and also why they fall short in producing the results we want to see when seasons change, when life gets hard, when culture shifts, when our personal doubts and fears collide with our circumstances.

The reason why our go-to resources fail us in the quest to be enough is because we don't sink our teeth into how we know that *he* absolutely is.

You see, even believers who heard the gospel firsthand from the apostles needed the reminder that their most fruitful works would flow out of the deepest reliance on redeeming grace. Because grace enables. Because grace secures our favor as his kids. Because God's grace is so astoundingly loving that we love him because he loved us first.

Listen, don't skip over this. Jesus loves you so much that he rescued you by grace. If you've received his gift through faith you

Right living
overflows from
right believing.

don't need to figure out how to be a model Christian, how to be more "on fire" for God, or even how to please God—if you're in Christ, you are already pleasing to him because of Jesus. Your number-one job as a believer is to return again and again to the good news of the gospel—the foundational truth of redeeming grace—and let it draw you near to him once again.

Don't forget it, don't dismiss it, don't sidestep it to get to the doing. You were made for good works, yes, but made first for relationship with God, who enables that work.

The grace we've been talking about—the grace that saves, rescues, redeems, and restores—is a grace that stokes the flames of orthopraxy *because* it is the pure unapologetic orthodoxy of salvation by grace alone. Right living overflows from right believing.

So when you see all the instructions in the gospel for how to live biblically, don't forget those instructions flow from the heart of a good Father whom you don't have to appease. What freedom when my kids hear my instructions to "look both ways before crossing the street" or "be kind to your brother" as instructions for their good and *because* they are loved and cared for already.

He's after your heart, friend. Don't forget.

He's your Father. The Savior who crossed the greatest divide there ever was in order to bring you back from the wreckage of sin and self-improvement is the same Father who seeks your joyful obedience because you know who he is. Because you know who you are. Because you love him back.

He isn't barking out orders or leaving you a checklist of dos and don'ts. Your loving Father has good work for you to do when you stop striving to produce the fruit on your own. Because of grace, we can walk in a manner worthy of him—as children who embody both light and heat.

ELEVEN

Grace Cancels Our Debt, For Real

Grace, grace, God's grace,
Grace that will pardon and cleanse within;
Grace, grace, God's grace,
Grace that is greater than all our sin!
—Julia H. Johnston, "Marvelous Grace of Our Loving Lord"

What are you doing, Ma?" I looked up from the mountain of cookware, small appliances, gift cards, and checks Troy and I had unwrapped after returning from our honeymoon. "I already have thank-you notes planned out for all these wedding gifts—you don't have to record them all again."

"No, *baobei*," she answered without missing a beat, "I'm

writing them down because, when it's our turn to send wedding gifts, we will gift in kind—or better—to show our appreciation and gratitude."

I hadn't brewed my first cup of coffee in my brand-new newlywed coffee maker, and I was already feeling the pressure to pay back the gift I was given.

I've since had to google whether this was a family or cultural thing, and it turns out the internet empathizes and validates my experience:

> A record is kept of how much each guest gives to the new-lyweds. This is done for several reasons. One reason is bookkeeping. . . . Another reason is that when unmarried guests eventually get married, the bride and groom are typically obliged to give the guest more money than what the newlyweds received at their wedding.[1]

This sense of owing and repayment wasn't new to me and didn't just appear while opening wedding gifts. It's a concept so ingrained in my Asian upbringing that I've caught myself missing the blessing of a friend paying for a meal for fear that I haven't fairly carried my weight. I've been known to overthink a gift exchange, worrying that mine was insufficient.

I have a new Asian American sister-friend named Jamie, who lives in the holy grail of Asian-food destinations: Orange County. For someone like me living in western Colorado, where there are no Asian grocery stores and ethnic cuisine is limited, Southern California offers everything my little Asian taste buds crave (don't get me wrong, we have amazing restaurants and my favorite sushi anywhere—shout-out to Pop Sushi in Durango,

Colorado). Chinese hot pot restaurants, boba and shaved ice dessert cafes, Korean BBQ, and Chinese bakeries, not to mention 99 Ranch Markets stocked with everything I never knew I needed to cook Asian cuisine.

So, when Jamie realized I had access to only what is available in the Asian aisle at Walmart for Chinese groceries, she offered to send me whatever I wanted from California. It wasn't convenient, and it wasn't expected. She simply did it out of love for me and my family.

My list was long: star anise, Chinese dry noodles, black vinegar, tapioca flour, Szechuan peppercorn peanuts that make your tongue numb, canned lychees, and grass jelly were just a few things to get her started. But then I also had items requested on the Trader Joe's run, since we don't have one of those, either, within a four-hour drive. Dried chili mangos, dill pickle popcorn, ghost pepper potato chips, everything bagel seasoning, and more dried chili mangos. She braved shopping during COVID-19, checked things off my list, and packed them all up in priority boxes.

It was like Christmas morning when we received our precious goods from the land of *douhua* and *baobing*.

But, unlike other errands and favors where receipts are turned in and money is quickly transferred, Jamie and I went back and forth for weeks before landing on the right amount for me to pay her back.

She sought to bless, and I didn't want to take that act of love from her, especially knowing our background as Asian American women who would never allow ourselves to lose face over outwardly keeping score or being the lesser giver. Left up to our upbringing, we ought to have maintained the norm: she'd insist on paying for it all, I'd insist on paying for it all, she'd win in her persistence, and I would allow it for *mianzi*'s sake and simply keep in the forefront of my mind that I owed her—*big*.

But, this time, I just couldn't—Asian cultural norms or not. Maybe someone else could have navigated the Asian dance better than I, but I knew I had too much baggage and too many issues with performance and striving to start a new friendship off wondering if I'd sufficiently met her expectations and relayed my gratitude. I cared more about having a real and honest relationship with her as my new friend than I cared about gratitude that looked like debt.

So, to give us both clarity and confidence moving forward, we agreed on what we would consider as the difference between a gift and a transaction. This was so helpful to me because for much of my life the two concepts have been muddy and intermingled. But there is a difference. One results in gratitude that owes nothing, and one is gratitude that pays what you owe. The oft unspoken division between giving and expecting something in return, between something being free and costly, between gift and debt, makes us constantly unsure of our relationships. We constantly doubt, feel our way around approval and relational favor, and sometimes even overcompensate for the debt we believe we owe if it's simply not clear where we stand.

I know some of my Asian American sisters are reading this right now nodding. But the truth is, regardless of whether you were brought up in the Deep South or in a first-generation immigrant family, all of us have been taught what is the proper and expected way to respond to undeserved kindness. Sometimes it helps to take notice of it by looking through another's cultural lens. I hope that's how it feels to look through mine because I want us to honestly deal with how debilitating it is when we fail to believe that grace is free.

As Jerry Bridges wrote:

> To the degree that we feel we are on a legal or performance relationship with God, to that degree our progress in sanctification is impeded. A legal mode of thinking gives indwelling sin an advantage, because nothing cuts the nerve of the desire to pursue holiness as much as a sense of guilt. On the contrary, nothing so motivates us to deal with sin in our lives as does the understanding and application of the two truths that our sins are forgiven and the dominion of sin is broken because of our union with Christ.[2]

We can't understand grace as the only means of true change in our lives if we don't fully grasp the extent of our forgiveness and pardon in Christ.

Striving doesn't simply look like keeping the law through good works or earning your salvation through right behavior. It can also look like constantly trying to repay the gift of grace with your offerings of holiness. It's being grateful for salvation but feeling so tethered to guilt and indebtedness that you miss the blessing and keep paying for the gift instead. I happen to have a cultural background that illustrated this clearly for me, but this is something a lot of us struggle with, isn't it?

For me, the struggle came full circle the day I read these words from John Piper in his book *Future Grace*:

> The debtor's ethic says, "Because you have done something good for me, I feel indebted to do something good for you." . . .

When our virtue—toward other people, or toward God—is born out of this sense of "paying back," we are in the grip of the debtor's ethic. . . . Subtly the gift is no longer a gift but a business transaction. And what was offered as free grace is nullified by distorted gratitude.[3]

Piper described a part of what had been plaguing my walk with Christ as a young believer. I could see it now—I was so busy trying to pay God back with holy behavior and good works, I was unknowingly stepping into legalistic shoes of a different kind—ones where I looked to right living and self-discipline as not merely the outworking of true faith but obligations to prove I was grateful for its existence in me. You may have encountered this kind of mindset too:

- If you love Jesus, you should sell everything and be a missionary.
- If you love Jesus, you should volunteer in the church.
- If you love Jesus, you should give back at least 10 percent of your earnings.

Listen—it's subtle. Serving as a missionary, volunteering at church, and tithing are all biblical ways to honor God, modeled for us through believers in Scripture. But the *should* is what turns a response in love to a response of debt. And the thing about debt is that it feels like a weight or a burden that hangs over your head until you've paid it off.

It feels like bills stacking up on the kitchen counter. It feels like owing a friend you haven't paid back. It feels like pressure to pay back a wedding gift before you've even begun to enjoy it.

The *should* is
what turns a
response in love
to a
response of debt.

More Than Cancelled Debt

I know what you're thinking: *Ruth, I've heard this all before. Yes, Jesus paid it all. I know that. But I'm still struggling with this mindset, and I need to feel freedom right now.* Hang in there with me, friend. Our feelings follow our foundational beliefs. We can't feel peace until we know peace. That's why this is so important to truly take in:

> And you, who were dead in your trespasses and the uncircumcision of your flesh, God made alive together with him, having forgiven us all our trespasses, by canceling the record of debt that stood against us with its legal demands. This he set aside, nailing it to the cross. (Col. 2:13–14)

If someone paid your mortgage today, handed you the free-and-clear deed to your home, you wouldn't send in a check this month to the mortgage company. You'd feel a burden lifted. You'd sit in gratitude. You'd be eager to enjoy your home. You'd wonder at the amazing kindness of a benefactor who took on your debt and paid it in full.

If we want to feel this same kind of freedom right now in our daily lives, we have to start with understanding the whole truth of the gospel.

The gospel is this: God sent Christ to live the perfect life that we couldn't live, and die the criminal death we deserved in our sin, so that we wouldn't just be freed from the debt we owed but granted eternal worthiness in his presence on account of Christ.

Simply put, the wonder of the gospel—that changes

everything if we believe it—is that our debts aren't just canceled; our account is filled to overflowing.

More than not empty, but overflowing.

More than tolerated, but highly favored.

More than pardoned, but adopted as family.

More than patched, but made new.

If you and I subscribe to a lesser idea of what the grace of God purchases for us, we've missed the good news.

So What About Guilt?

So how exactly do we get off course from this glorious truth? We're all taught this gospel of grace as young believers, but somewhere along the way the Enemy leads us back into self-reliance. How do we watch out for this? What does the Enemy use to deceive us? I hope you hear me loud and clear: believing only one piece of the gospel is what keeps us from true freedom.

We can believe that we are saved by grace, but if we stop there and think we are indebted until we've sufficiently paid our dues, it will not be saving grace we hope in but a false gospel.

We can believe that our sins are forgiven, but if we stop there without considering the ongoing sin this side of heaven, we will lack the gospel hope of holiness—not just forgiveness.

We can believe that there's a place for us in heaven, but if we stop there, we miss the benefits of eternal life in God's presence with us right now, through the Holy Spirit (John 17:3).

You see, we can't just take hold of one part of the gospel and still know the full gospel; the good news affects so much more than simply a transaction or transfer from bad to good,

Believing only
one piece of the gospel
is what keeps us
from
true freedom.

hell-bound to heavenward. In fact, the gospel reshapes everything about every mundane, ordinary moment in between.

I wrote meditations for everyday worship in my book *Beholding and Becoming* for this very reason; the gospel will transform us in our everyday lives if we stop living according to our circumstances and instead live aligned to awe and worship of God. Our striving and anxious bent toward proving our worth with God and with others are not only special-occasion struggles; they accompany us throughout the quiet, unseen moments of our daily lives.

When we struggle with guilt and not-enoughness, we wrestle in secret. For me, my most condemning, fearful thoughts most often rise to the surface after the kids are in bed, when the day is done, when I'm recounting the regrets and mishaps of the day. What gospel are you preaching to yourself in the corners of your mind where the Enemy has sought to pronounce guilt and condemnation? You need to preach the whole gospel if you are to combat a thorough Enemy of lies.

But if you've read your Bible you know what Paul said about the state of our guilt as believers. Notice that Paul wasn't preaching a partial gospel to us. He was reminding us of who we are and why we don't stand condemned when he said, "There is therefore now no condemnation for those who are in Christ Jesus. For the law of the Spirit of life has set you free in Christ Jesus from the law of sin and death" (Rom. 8:1–2).

I want to lean in and say something with care just for a moment here:

Some of us have done things that make our stomachs turn when all the distractions fade and we have an opportunity to think about them. Regret maybe feels like just the tip of the iceberg for you. This topic of self-condemnation feels tricky, if not impossible, to navigate. Or, perhaps, there are lasting consequences for the choices you've made, and the reality of those consequences taunt you day in and day out. The idea that there is "no condemnation" feels hardly feasible when you feel so defined by the failures in your life.

And if you're like me, the details of those poor and sometimes costly decisions are difficult to forget, even if they are a thing of the past, as you replay your mistakes over and over in your mind. Perhaps your sin involved another human being, and you've sought forgiveness and reconciled. Maybe things are "fine," but you haven't forgiven yourself.

I just want you to know that I have regrets too. I have shameful chapters I wish weren't part of my story. I, too, have experienced consequences of my sin—great and small—long after I knew I was forgiven. And I want you to know: the reason why Paul, the man who once held the coats of those who stoned Stephen for preaching the gospel (Acts 22:20), could unswervingly declare that there is now no condemnation for those found in Christ is because grace is infinitely greater than our sin and shame. Surrendering to Christ did not erase his past; it rewrote his future.

Friend, we cannot pay back an infinitely more capable, more generous God. Anything we'd even attempt to offer back to him was given to us in the first place. The psalmist in Psalm 116 declared his love for the Lord and recounted all the kindness and mercy God had shown him. And in the midst of feeling overwhelmed by all that God had done, he asked a question and answered it for himself. "What shall I render to the LORD for all his benefits to me? I will lift up the cup of salvation and call on the name of the LORD" (vv. 12–13).

The psalmist could not repay God or "render" to him

anything worthy of all that God had done. He could simply drink deeply of God's rescue and long for more. He offered back to God the very thing God desires—our desire for him and for his glory to be made known in and through us.

The only hope we have for *feeling* the freedom of a debt canceled and paid for, and believing we are no longer condemned, is to continually dwell and rest in the exceedingly greater power of God's love to rescue us. To drink of his cup of salvation and turn to no other. Just as this beloved hymn reminds us:

> *Marvelous grace of our loving Lord,*
> *Grace that exceeds our sin and our guilt!*
> *Yonder on Calvary's mount out-poured—*
> *There where the blood of the Lamb was spilt.*
> *[Refrain]*
> *Grace, grace, God's grace,*
> *Grace that will pardon and cleanse within;*
> *Grace, grace, God's grace,*
> *Grace that is greater than all our sin!*[4]

What do we owe God? We owe him nothing of payment and everything in surrender. We owe nothing out of guilt and everything in gratitude. We owe nothing that he did not give us in the first place, which indeed is everything.

And so, read the first question of the *Westminster Shorter Catechism* anew if you haven't recently, or even if it's brand new to you:

Q: What is the chief end of man?
A: To glorify God, and to enjoy Him forever.[5]

God's redemption story of his creation—starring Jesus—and the grace by which he brings us back to himself is a debt-free restoration project. It's not a low-interest loan or a thirty-year mortgage—generous but far from free. We were created to fellowship with God and reflect him. We've been given every reason to give thanks and to enjoy all he's provided for us.

Everything—even our grateful praise—belongs to God. And grace? Grace makes it possible for us to stop keeping score, stop keeping track, and stop the fear of not paying back what we've been given.

Open the gift, friend. It's yours, and you needn't worry about writing that thank-you card to show your appreciation. I promise, if you take the gift of grace as yours, you won't be able to help but desire more and love God in return. It's what he purposed for grace to do. And if you already have received the gift, enjoy him to the fullest. Don't hold back.

TWELVE

Grace Rewrites Our Stories

If we find ourselves with a desire that nothing in this world can satisfy, the most probable explanation is that we were made for another world.

—C. S. Lewis

This book sounded like a good idea to write until it became difficult and tender to unearth the personal and spiritual undercurrents that have swept me along most of my life. To wrestle with my own journey from self-striving to grace was to confront the reasons I've turned to striving so often in my life. The truth is, we strive when we long for something we believe will pull us out of despair and into a sense of fulfillment. We strive to make our dreams come true. Sometimes those are tangible dreams like starting a business, being debt free, or earning a doctorate. But sometimes those dreams are intangibles like finding love, feeling accepted, or being happy with who you are.

So much of my self-striving was an effort to iron out the wrinkles in my story that left me conflicted inside. Carefully pressed pleats can hide the parts you don't want to see in any garment. Striving was my incessant pursuit of perfect pleats, but grace ran me through the wash and released the wrinkles I couldn't hide on my own.

I was recently in Nashville, in a room with some of the most inspiring authors, Bible teachers, and gospel-centered song-writers I know, working on a wonderfully collaborative project together. To get us warmed up for the day, our friend Sarah led us in an exploratory prompted writing exercise. We were to write down whatever flowed out in fifteen minutes from the prompt "I am from . . ."

Here's what I wrote:

> I am from minced garlic and scallions, fried up in oil—
> where everything good begins.
> I am from a homeland I can't see in my mind's eye.
> I am from secrets and expectations and the right way to
> never let anyone down.
> I am from crescent dumplings and long noodles—long
> life, but why?
> I am from downplayed individualism, where boys are
> treasured over girls with something to prove.
> I am from prosperity, dreams, guilt, and fear.

I am from Chinese ink and perfectly held brushes.
I am from "conform and don't make waves."
I am from the boat that crossed the ocean—the great
divide . . .
  . . . from lost to found,
  . . . from treading and staying afloat to
clinging to a lifeline.
I am from the little red envelope you don't deserve to the
name in the book in permanent ink.

I scratched out these words—unedited—as a stream of consciousness on a page in my journal. And as we read our fifteen-minute collections of thoughts, some of us cried.

There's something telling about the words you use to describe your underpinnings. "I am from . . ." What makes you, you? What informs your thoughts? What shapes your identity?

Some of our *from* stories are painful. They include details and happenings that we wish didn't exist. That would never have been a part of what we planned for our lives. And because of these wrinkles in our stories, we take intentional steps to not continue in the creases of pain in our lives. We make future plans built around a refusal to continue on from where we've been. And sometimes that is a good and true course of action.

But other times our plans can be a form of escape. We can work to avoid any further wrinkling by attempting to create a smooth and seamless story ahead. A desire to control and direct the outcome of our lives in a way that will obscure the pain of the past or help us forget it altogether. It's not difficult to hope in a well-considered, well-executed plan—to hope for change, a better set of circumstances, new opportunities.

The only thing is, no matter how perfectly you and I nail that job interview or research where to move, no matter how much we level up or how well we map out the five-year plan, you and I can't control how our lives turn out. At least not the way the self-actualization moguls would have us believe.

Just look at 2020. Plans obliterated before dated and color-coded planners even had opportunities to show bent corners or coffee spills on frequented pages.

If we hope—place our happiness or sense of well-being—in our plans, we will be derailed when a circumstance, season, or an entire year doesn't make sense.

The Tension of Our Circumstances

When I trace my story back to its origins with my grandparents and parents, I find messy, twisted roots that are difficult to unravel and understand. Most of our stories are like that. My dad was born on a boat somewhere between the coast of China and Taiwan. My parents met and married in Taiwan after both of their parents fled China in 1949 to escape communism. My grandmother never saw her mother again, and most of my family history is lost or not spoken of.

I can't imagine what my grandparents experienced, *endured*, escaping the tyranny of their homeland during political unrest in China. It certainly wasn't what they had planned for their lives. They left all they knew in hopes of better. They did this twice, as both sets of grandparents eventually moved to the United States. And in time, my parents joined them in the United States, but their hopes and dreams didn't come to fruition either. Their

If we hope in our *plans*, we will be **derailed** when a circumstance, *season*, or an entire year doesn't make sense.

plans included university degrees, financial stability, and close family ties. Instead their story was filled with twists and turns of conflict, hurt, loss, and ultimately unfulfilled dreams.

We all have stories of painful family history and its implications in our lives, both hidden and revealed. I've learned from experience and conviction that digging up details and talking about them, in and of itself, isn't what frees us. We have to read the story God's written into our lives through the language and lens of God's Word. That language and that lens is the love of God—a love that pursues, rescues, redeems, and restores. These stories— our hard stories—don't exist to highlight our ability to excavate the pits but to show off God's amazing grace to lift us out.

We are caught between two worlds in more ways than we know. Some of us are literally navigating changes we didn't anticipate and the feeling of displacement. Some of us are between two worlds of who we were before Christ and who we want to be in Christ. Some of us are navigating the tension of being the child yet being the parent. And most of us feel the tension between trusting God and trying to control everything for our own good.

We are between two worlds—the spiritual and the temporal.

Between two worlds—the seen and unseen.

Between two worlds—who we think others expect us to be and who we know ourselves to be.

Between two worlds—the intersection of *what we planned* and *how things really are.* And right in the middle of our plans not turning out the way we hoped and our inability to see God's purposes is where the grace of God changes us, even if it doesn't change our circumstances.

Grace is not a Band-Aid for our hard questions, unresolved

heartaches, unwanted waiting, and broken dreams. But God's grace does inform how we make sense of the journey when our stories don't turn out the way we expected or hoped.

I'm reminded of how the Israelites waited longingly for the promise of redemption to come to fruition. The plan was for the Messiah to rule and reign, and for salvation to come to the Jews. They envisioned freedom, victory, relief from their oppressors. In Hebrews 11:13–16—the famous "faith chapter"—the writer recorded the acts of faith from those who stepped into God's story of redemption, though they didn't know or see its final outcome:

> These all died in faith, not having received the things promised, but having seen them and greeted them from afar, and having acknowledged that they were strangers and exiles on the earth. For people who speak thus make it clear that they are seeking a homeland. If they had been thinking of that land from which they had gone out, they would have had opportunity to return. But as it is, they desire a better country, that is, a heavenly one. Therefore God is not ashamed to be called their God, for he has prepared for them a city.

These servants used of God—Abraham, Moses, Jacob, David, and more—never experienced the full plan revealed. They had to trust God's purposes even when the plan did not seem to deliver the results they believed best at the time they thought most necessary.

Can you imagine how they may have felt? If I were in their same position, I'd likely fuss:

"I thought you said, Lord . . ."
"It's not supposed to be like this."

"Why don't I get to see what happens next?"

"Why didn't everything go as planned—as I planned?"

This is just a small sampling of what I sound like when I'm thrown off by my circumstances or frustrated when my hard work doesn't amount to seeing the results I believe I deserve.

How does the grace of God affect the way we live right now—right this minute—when we can't control our past or our future? Is it possible to stop striving and rest in God's grace when you feel *unrest* in the tension of your circumstances?

I think the answer to those questions can be found in the admonition Peter gave to believers in exile who were far from home. The dispersed believers in the early church were not unlike those of us who are living as redeemed in a fallen world. Peter opened his letter by turning his readers' attention to their hope in heaven and the salvation that is theirs even when living as foreigners and aliens in the land. Rather than just telling believers that they should tough it out and not let their circumstances beat them down, he instead reminded them that they already had a treasure that all those before them—including the very ones the writer of Hebrews talked about—longed for and waited to see revealed.

He reminded them that grace was their hope and assurance in the midst of trials and suffering.

The believers who received Peter's letter were between two worlds and not at home. Choosing to follow Christ didn't make for a smooth or comfortable journey in the ancient world. Being a Christian was costly and certainly not a self-improvement plan from the standpoint of societal acceptance and approval. As believers who had direct access to those who witnessed the resurrection of Christ, you'd think they would have had some version of tireless hope and perspective. Nope, they were in exile, and nothing about their stories, according to their circumstances, looked privileged, special, or very grace-laced. So Peter began his letter reminding them that they'd been born again into a hope and an inheritance that couldn't be taken away. He then said:

> In this you rejoice, though now for a little while, if necessary, you have been grieved by various trials, so that the tested genuineness of your faith—more precious than gold that perishes though it is tested by fire—may be found to result in praise and glory and honor at the revelation of Jesus Christ. (1 Peter 1:6–7)

Peter's exhortation right from the start was for believers to recognize the privilege it is to be recipients of grace—grace revealed, grace received, grace applied, and grace sustained. It's a grace that enables the hope that sustains us in times of uncertainty, pain, and when our lives don't look the way we hoped or expected. God's grace isn't an afterthought for a believer walking through unexpected circumstances; it's the anchor. And in the midst of this encouragement, Peter said a curious thing about this grace that we're talking about.

> Concerning this salvation, the prophets who prophesied about the grace that was to be yours searched and inquired carefully, inquiring what person or time the Spirit of Christ in them was indicating when he predicted the sufferings of Christ and the subsequent glories. It was revealed to them that they were serving not themselves but you, in the things that have now

been announced to you through those who preached the good news to you by the Holy Spirit sent from heaven, things into which angels long to look. (vv. 10–12)

The thing that sticks out for me when I read Peter's words here is that God chooses to use each of us in the bigger story he's writing of redemption and rescue. We don't get to choose how we are used, when we are used, and what part we will play. It's not about us just like it was not about the early Christians. God's grace was revealed in God's timing, and we get to be recipients of it.

> *On this side of the cross,* where we now know the death, burial, and resurrection of Jesus . . .
> *On this side of the cross,* where we understand that the Law and the commands from the Lord were never able to be fully met in us, but only in Christ . . .
> *On this side of the cross,* where we learn that the obligation to holiness is enabled by the work of the Holy Spirit . . .
> *On this side of the cross,* where we realize that God was foretelling his way of salvation through the picture of the Israelites escaping slavery and crossing the Red Sea . . .
> *On this side of the cross,* where we find all of history changed because God is merciful . . .
> *On this side of the cross,* we see clearly—or at least we have every opportunity to see clearly—the full picture of God's amazing grace in the work of Christ. This is what the angels longed to see.

And yet where are we looking? Too often I'm not looking at what has been revealed as God's purpose but rather at what I don't

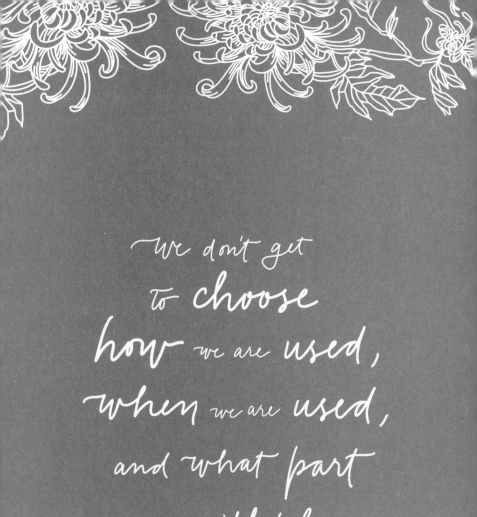

We don't get
to **choose**
how we are *used*,
when we are *used*,
and what part
we will play.

understand of my past. I'm so preoccupied with the plans I made and how I want to orchestrate their fruition that I miss the grand and glorious benefit of being held by and through grace. God's purposes, his plans, and the good of his people always work together in unison. As Paul the Apostle wrote in Romans 8:28: "And we know that for those who love God all things work together for good, for those who are called according to his purpose."

There's a reason why this verse—this declaration that has been terribly overused to assuage bad choices and dating indecision—comes in the middle of Romans 8, right between the wonder of being adopted into God's family as an heir no longer condemned and the assurance that nothing in all the world can separate us from the love of God. It is so extraordinary not simply on account of the cherry-on-top blessing that God works things together for good but rather because of the unshakeable foundation that makes the blessing secure: God calls us according to his purpose.

The latter part of Romans 8 would have no legs to stand on apart from the foundation of the first. When the grace of God is our true good, we don't have to hope in all things working together in the way that seems right to us; we can want him and love him instead.

We Are Not Our Own

Our place as sons and daughters settles our present and our future. It designates us as partakers of the life-transforming benefits of grace. Children who feel secure enough to call God "Abba, Father" are not worrying about securing their own good by their own means. If we strive to make our dreams come true, we cease striving when our greatest needs are fulfilled in Christ.

When Caleb, my oldest son, wanders downstairs in the morning before any of the other boys are awake, embraces his dad, and vulnerably confides in him about his discouragement and need for counsel, he is coming to Troy as a son—as one who believes his father has only good in mind for him. Caleb trusts in Troy's counsel and seeks his wisdom because he knows his own limitations in making sense of whatever he is struggling with. And so it should be for us with God.

You see, the more a daughter knows the faithfulness and greatness of her father, the more she will desire his purposes over her own plans.

"According to the will of God."

"According to his purposes."

Those are sweet—not scary—words to those who trust in Christ.

Sister, striving to secure your good, comfortable, pain-avoiding future is the way of death and soul-crippling anxiety. The swirling and fretting over how to avoid hardship and only experience good is all a manifestation of what is at the core: our desire for control. Yes, we're literally told by books and movies and podcasts that if we can rescue ourselves and write our own stories, we will have the results we want and the good life we desire. But we've bought into a lie.

Can I restate what we see again and again in Scripture? The good life isn't the absence of heartache; it's the presence of God, by grace, in the midst of it. Our hope in the midst of hardship is that Jesus doesn't just work things out for our good—he *is* our good.

And like the early believers in exile, our "I am from . . ." pales in comparison to "Who I am and what I have in Christ." The dots in your life can connect in the messiest of ways, or you may not yet know how they connect at all. Scattered and dispersed believers in Peter's day were told to hold fast to their inheritance in Christ—the grace that was already theirs. What matters most, for us who are walking out stories not yet fully written, is to do the same.

When we replace self-striving with life-transforming grace, we declare that we are not our own, but God's. And when we are his, his purposes prevail for our good and his glory. The unfolding of his ways is always more than we ask or imagine for those who realize that God has already done the impossible through salvation (Eph. 3:20). If he can cross the greatest divide to secure our place in his presence forever, even the most difficult detours or unexpected changes of plan are not impossible for God to redeem.

Grafted In

My dad tells me that when their hopes and dreams were shattered in the wake of unexpected trials that first year in the United States, an unlikely blessing came in the form of a man they called Brother Jim. Jim gathered refugees and immigrants, housing them and aiding them as they worked to make a life in this country. Jim was a believer and took my parents to church on Sundays. I don't know what he looked like, his ethnicity, or what made my parents trust him enough to live with him for an entire year before moving to the Southwest, but he's the reason I'm called

Ruth. And how fitting—to ultimately receive the namesake of one who was also a foreigner trying to adjust to her new home. One who trusted God through all the tragedies of her life and surrendered instead to his plans for her. From the line of that Ruth came the savior of the world. Because God chose to give us a savior through the line of a woman who trusted God with her story, even when things did not go as planned or as wanted, I'm no longer one who can only resort to bending and pleasing others.

For all the times I've complained and fussed about my name, wishing Brother Jim had suggested Kimberly, Jennifer, or Ashley (you know, some name that would've earned me popularity points in the early eighties), I'm grateful that I get to tell the story of how that name came to be. I can see it better now than ever before: that even when I have walked through times and seasons that felt like exile, God was always writing a story in my life that was more than I could imagine. That would later challenge my misconceptions about belonging, home, welcome, and identity. About my plans and perspectives versus his. He's a good Father like that.

For all the ways that some of us have felt orphaned—even with parents and various branches on the family tree—we can trace our roots back from the fruit of faith today and realize the power of being grafted into the family of God. The amazing way God indeed works all things—things we don't expect, want, or think we're able to handle—together for good.

God's plan was never for us to be alone, without a country, without a home, without roots. Our "I am from . . ." was never meant to be penned with anything but the heart of God. But the grace of God—the mighty and powerfully transforming grace of God—restores what is broken, brings us home, grafts us in, and makes us fit to abide with Christ and him with us. It was his plan all along, and amazing grace makes us able to want his story most of all.

THIRTEEN

Grace Replaces Fear with Freedom

For God has not given us a spirit of fear, but of
power and of love and of a sound mind.
—2 TIMOTHY 1:7 NKJV

It's nine o'clock in the morning, and I'm hitting the ground running with all that's waiting for me today—including the final chapters of this book. And just like so many previous seasons of my life, my temptation is to default to fear when stressors and pressure are near.

What if I can't get this done on time?
What if I drop the ball?

What if everyone's disappointed in me?
What if I make a fool of myself trying?
What if God is frustrated with my fear?
What if I'm not enough for this?
What if my asking "what if" means I'm not even a
   Christian? (Bonus lie for when you're really in a tailspin
   of fear.)

Isn't it just like the Enemy to repeat the same tricks he started with at the beginning, using our fears to cause us to question: Is God really enough? Is he holding out on me? Is he really trustworthy?

And as I sit down to write to you today, I'm faced with the perpetual need for realignment with freedom instead of fear. Striving is such a familiar way of self-preservation that it doesn't take much—a few stressful emails, a chaotic home, a pressing deadline, costly home repairs—to put me out of alignment with truth. Like a hip out of place or a crick in your neck that feels stuck after a bad night's sleep, we can't properly walk in the manner worthy of Christ if we are out of alignment. We need daily adjustments.

As I mentioned earlier, I'm a fan of one and done. Nothing irritates me more than having to repeat myself, redo a task that I've already done and checked off my list, ask the kids to pick up their toys (again), or persist at something I wish worked like a one-time activation fee.

Exercise, for example. Does it really need to be regular? Must it take thirty days of consistency to establish a new pattern or to see measurable results?

Can't I work out one *really* solid time at the beginning of the year—let's say January 1, along with clean eating and portion control for the day—and be good for the remaining 364 days left in the year? Why does establishing routines in health and fitness take practice and persistence? Why must it require ongoing deliberate choices to say yes to some things and no to others?

I jest (or do I?) and I betray my weakness here. But it's true. I love efficiency, and I hate slow results. I love blooms, right now. I don't want to have to prune and plant and weed and wait. But as I've said for a long time, #youdonthavetobebloomingtobegrowing.

True change is made up of a million small, daily, seemingly insignificant choices. The course we take is determined by the minute pivots we make in the direction of our hearts' desires and core beliefs. As in, if your heart is fixed on fear, your actions will be directed by self-preservation. If your heart is steadied on the approval you can attain, you will be constantly directed by others' opinions of you. But if you, instead, find your assurance in who God says you are by the work of grace, your responses will reflect what you value most—what God has done for you.

If that sounds familiar, it should. I spent quite a bit of time on this topic in my book *Beholding and Becoming*, but here I want to make it clear:

This is not passive; we have to fight for this.

I want you to know that realigning your mind, heart, and identity to *grace, not works* is a daily battle. Don't be surprised when it's minute by minute. Don't be surprised when it's not instant change. Don't be surprised when you find yourself needing, once again, to speak against the Enemy's taunts of discouragement, doubt, and derailing fear.

What are the stressors that reveal your natural propensities toward striving and control in response to fear and doubt? Where do you see the old pattern of earning and proving rear its ugly head, even after you know that you've been saved by grace through faith?

I'm sure it's abundantly obvious after the first half of this book, but my striving is always connected to fear of not meeting expectations—which for me is connected to the fear of not being loved, which is connected to a fear of lacking worth. Whew. Fear is a ruthless beast we won't just overcome with peppy affirmations and grit; we overcome fear with something more powerful, more capable of filling the void, more sustaining than any outrunning of it could produce.

Fear is overcome with freedom—the freedom purchased for us in love through Christ's grace.

But if grace is so amazing, it ought to change us; it ought to make a difference when we are anxious; it ought to direct our longings and desires toward what they ought to love, right?

If grace really changes everything, then living fearlessly in the grace of God should come easily, right?

It should, and it does. But the Enemy, Satan, isn't called the Accuser for nothing:

> In times of adversity Satan will seek to plant the thought in our minds that God is angry with us and is disciplining us out of wrath. Here is another instance when we need to preach the gospel to ourselves. It is the gospel that will reassure that the penalty for our sins has been paid, that God's justice has been fully satisfied. It is the gospel that supplies a good part of the armor of God with which we are to stand against the accusing attacks of the Devil (see Ephesians 6:13–17).[1]

Fear
is
overcome
with
freedom.

Satan's very favorite tactic, from the beginning, has been to mess with our minds and to plant seeds of doubt in God's faithfulness, God's forgiveness, and God's favor.

This is the trifecta of freedom in a believer's life. His faithfulness eclipses our clawing for control; his forgiveness erases debilitating guilt and shame; and his favor eradicates our need to look anywhere else for love than God himself.

If only Satan was like the comedy sketches suggest: a tiny, pudgy mischief maker in red tights, holding a pitchfork, who sits comfortably on your shoulder. But he's the father of lies and not even obvious ones. He's the father of the small whispers, the feelings that haunt us, and the frenzy of thoughts that creep in and take over our minds. You can squash a Tinker Bell–sized madman with horns; you can't fight the Deceiver with strength and might. You must fight his lies with truth.

Lie: God is only faithful to the faithful—those who keep their end of the deal.
Truth: God's grace is displayed in that he is faithful even when we are faithless (2 Tim. 2:13).

Lie: God will only forgive those who get their acts together.
Truth: We are forgiven by grace because we will never get our acts together on our own (Rom. 5:8).

Lie: God's favor is uncertain; there's no way to know he's not mad at you.
Truth: We have the assurance of God's favor when we are saved by grace because his grace is his favor (Rom. 8:30–31).

If, as Christ followers, we were to cling to what is true about God's faithfulness, forgiveness, and favor, we'd be unstoppable for the kingdom of God.

> Unstoppable in our ability to comfort others rather than be absorbed in ourselves.
> Unstoppable in using our God-given gifts without comparison and self-assessment.
> Unstoppable in proclaiming where our hope comes from to a hopeless world around us.
> Unstoppable in offering others the same grace we've received from God.
> Unstoppable in mercy.
> Unstoppable in speaking a kind word when someone deserves otherwise.
> Unstoppable in living life to the fullest and wasting nothing, not even our suffering.

You see, believers who let nothing through the gates of their minds but a never-ending loop of God's faithfulness, forgiveness, and favor will be defensible against the Enemy from any direction.

A believer anchored thus is a triple threat, which is exactly why the Enemy is so persistent to instill doubt in all three.

Even Jesus was allowed to be tempted by Satan, whose very first words to him were, "If you are the Son of God" (Matt. 4:3). "If"? *If?*

Or recall his opening line to Eve in the garden: "Did God really say . . . ?" (Gen. 3:1 NIV).

As J. D. Greear said, "Satan puts question marks in your life where God has put periods."[2] Those question marks drive us back to the false promises of striving in our own strength and striving *for* ourselves.

Secure Identity

Until my forties, I struggled consistently to like my face. I remember when Ashlee Simpson undoubtedly altered her nose and I was simultaneously horrified and a little envious. Or when it became a thing for Asian women to have eyelid surgery or use eyelid tape to solve the "problem" of a monolid. And then there was me—with one hooded eye and one double-lidded eye.

I don't know exactly when or how it was that an Asian American girl with mismatched lids, silky, jet-black hair, and naturally tanned unblemished skin started thinking herself completely inadequate because she didn't have blonde hair, hazel eyes, and a button nose. Was it when she was told her face was round "like a clock"? Or that her nose was "flat"? Or when her eyes were called "slits"? Or when she was told she has no eyelashes? Or maybe it was when no makeup instruction, foundation colors, or beauty books ever applied to someone who looked like her—at least not in the early nineties.

I wasn't born doubting the way God constructed my facial features. I saw myself differently because there was an ongoing loop of lies serving as the soundtrack of my youth.

"She's so pretty she doesn't even look Chinese." These words weren't meant to be hurtful; they were simply spoken by someone from a passing generation and a different perspective. But they hurt me as a young woman still trying to feel comfortable in her own skin.

Lies don't have to attack every area of our lives to be effective; they need only chip away at what we haven't settled once and for all.

Let's talk about the lies we tell ourselves—because here's where the rubber meets the road with our grace-not-striving, faith-not-works, amazing-God-instead-of-amazing-me journey.

Let's talk about all the ways we can put a bookmark in a book like this, close it, and walk away chewing on how we want to be realigned with what really makes us pleasing to God but then, by the time we've answered a few urgent text messages, checked Instagram a few times, and finished loading the dishwasher, find ourselves forgetful and returning to the same old operating system of answering our sense of lack with *prove-I-am-enough-ness.*

I want to show you how I revisit and rehearse the benefits of grace when my natural, sinful self is ready to buy into the next lie I want to believe. In case you've missed this, I want to restate it here:

We are—in our sin nature—wired for self-improvement that depends on us, not God.

We are—in our sin nature—wired to fret over our own images instead of reflecting his.

We are—in our sin nature—wired to believe God's holding out on us and needs us to look out for ourselves.

And we are—in our sin nature—wired to welcome the lie that we are beggars and not heirs in the kingdom of God.

Grace is the means by which God rewires our souls and redeems us from our "natural" inclinations. The temptation to believe lies is not the exception but the rule.

In the rolling waves of continual self-improvement, any lie about who we are or who God is only needs to find the tender places of "If?" and "Did God really say . . . ?" to make a fearful striver out of any one of us.

So we need to sit up and pay attention to how Jesus answered Satan with what the Word of God says. Jesus, who came as the conduit of redeeming grace himself, opposed the lies of the Enemy with biblical truth. He didn't mess around; he went straight to the defense of what God had already settled. And we must do the same.

Without the transforming grace of God, we would have no answer for the Accuser but our own feelings, our own track records, or our own confidence. We'd be tossed about in fear and doubt because, quite frankly, we just can't outsmart him with our own resources. But by grace, through faith, our defense is Jesus Christ—we don't answer for ourselves. While self-help teaches us to rely on ourselves, Jesus sets the example (even as God's Son!) for us to anchor our hope and defense in the Word of God.

A Sound Mind

"For God has not given us a spirit of fear, but of power and of love and of a sound mind" (1 Tim. 1:7 NKJV).

A sound mind—the battleground for applying and living into the benefits of grace.

Like my friend Jennie Allen said, "The greatest spiritual battle of our generation is being fought between our ears."[3]

Paul's instruction at the start of Romans 12 to "be transformed by the renewing of your mind" (v. 2 NIV) is far from soft or sentimental. I read these as fighting words—words that defensively place a believer's confidence in redeeming grace into action.

Do you see why it matters so much where our confidence lies and not just what we do in response to the Enemy's attacks? There's no renewing of the mind if you don't know what to fix your mind on. Paul sought to make sure we would not be flummoxed about such things and took all the previous chapters in Romans to make it clear for us.

Renewing our minds with the truth of our salvation leads to transformation and steadiness of thought, and therein lies the secret to fighting the spirit of fear with the spirit of power and love.

Without the grounding pillars of grace—our great need, God's sovereign rescue, Jesus' substitution, and the Holy Spirit's sustaining—we'd have little to stand on but our feeble attempts at conquering fear and facing our failures.

A sound mind and secure identity in Christ together anchor us to the realities of what grace has accomplished for us—even when we can't *yet see* all that grace will one day transform in us. Said another way: "What Christ is doing *in you* is still incomplete. But in what Jesus Christ has done *for you* there is not a single tiny crack that the satanic arrows can penetrate."[4]

So speak to the Enemy's arrows of doubt and destruction with truth. Borrow these words I speak if it helps get you started:

By grace, through faith, Christ has already freed me from my chains. Your doubts and threats can only lead me to strive anxiously and will never offer me the assurance that grace secures.

Don't try to battle Satan's devious, almost-like-the-real-thing-but-not ideas with fluffy platitudes and self-affirming motivational talks. They don't stand and, I'd argue, sometimes are used and twisted to form chains that hold us down rather than release us. The heart-swelling anthems proclaiming, "Self-love is your superpower," "Believe in yourself," or "You're worthy of everything you desire" fall flat and fail to deliver. The currency of self-assurance is confidence, backed only by your own greatness (or belief that you are great). But the currency of being truly enough is God's favor through grace, backed by a God who sacrificed his son, Jesus, to pay the price of our rescue.

This is the great exchange that nullifies our need to be the greatest.

This is the beautiful story of freedom you must tell your soul when it's off the rails.

Tell your soul where you were, what God did to save you, how he freed you from your chains, and why you can stop your worry, fear, and doubt.

If you know me, you know I love old hymns—for the accuracy with which they preach the gospel to my heart and the efficiency through which they deliver it memorably. Maybe Charles Wesley penned "And Can It Be That I Should Gain?" to tell the good news to himself because he was prone to forget as well.

Long my imprisoned spirit lay,
Fast bound in sin and nature's night,
Thine eye diffused a quick'ning ray,
I woke, the dungeon flamed with light;
My chains fell off, my heart was free;
I rose, went forth and followed Thee.

I'm done with
treading water
when the
shores of grace
are
mine to dwell on.

No condemnation now I dread;
Jesus, and all in Him is mine!
Alive in Him, my living Head,
And clothed in righteousness divine,
Bold I approach th'eternal throne,
And claim the crown, through Christ my own.[5]

Fear, doubt, and condemnation won't cease to exist this side of heaven. But we do get to choose who we will listen to. We get to decide what will fill our minds and inform our identities.

When the lights fade, the worship music stops playing, and no one is standing by to deliver a word of encouragement, we can either wander aimlessly back into the whispers of inadequacy and shouts of condemnation or stand firm on the grace that both saves and defends us against the Enemy's lies. We can tell our actions to follow our renewed minds. Friend, I'm done with treading water when the shores of grace are mine to dwell on.

You too?

FOURTEEN

Grace Makes
Forgiveness Possible

*Gratitude and murmuring never abide in the
same heart at the same time.*
—E. M. Bounds

The stories we tell ourselves about how we are loved or not loved, guilty or forgiven, rescued or perishing—these are the stories that tell us to either strive for self-improvement or rest in life-transforming grace. These are the stories that either shape our understanding of the gospel or become reshaped themselves in our minds through the lens of the gospel. The latter is what we're working toward in this journey together.

I hope you're beginning to see how God's grace changes

everything, even the stories you tell yourself *about* yourself. And when we start seeing our stories and our circumstances through the lens of the gospel, we realize that grace changes the stories we tell ourselves about others as well.

We talked about a sound mind in the previous chapter, and now I want to show you how grace transforms the way you seek to change other people. I don't know about you, but nothing proves my true convictions like action—like what I actually do, not just say I believe. Our actions, big and small, and *how* we choose to live what we believe, prove that the grace of God is not a convenient accessory in our lives—but a lifeline.

I've spent a good amount of time here sharing glimpses of my history and how I've crumbled under the weight of self-inflicted or socially inflicted ideas of performing up to standard. If I'm honest, sometimes I find myself wielding the same law that couldn't save me on others, as if they can perform their way to pleasing when I cannot. Turns out, we're obsessed with improving others as much as we're driven to improve ourselves.

Perfecting *everything* is really our natural modus operandi, as we've seen again and again, for avoiding pain, disappointment, and heartache. Isn't that really the heart of it, still?

But the truth is, we simply aren't enough—perfect enough, all-knowing enough, good enough, wise enough—to orchestrate the kind of life that won't let us down. *Or to orchestrate the kind of relationships that won't let us down.* (Psst, that really is the good news of the gospel, because God promises to never let us down or let us go.)

I don't know about you, but even in knowing that this is true, I can, in my sin, act as if it's up to me to make all things and all people think, behave, feel, and do as they should.

I can always identify my tendency to fix others like I want to fix myself through the words I wield and the mental records I keep. And by mental records, I don't just mean the way my nine-year-old knows exactly the number of jellybeans his other brothers had while he was taking out the trash. I don't mean keeping track of whose turn it is to pick the movie tonight. And I don't just mean that I'm good at remembering who should pay for dinner. Truth be told, these are the minor leagues.

I'm referring to another well-developed skill:

- I can forget lots of important dates, but I rarely forget what she said in anger.
- I can't keep track of my keys, but I know exactly where and when he betrayed my trust.
- I'm better at remembering a record of wrongs than I am at recalling the good.
- I'm good at keeping score, friends, and I'm not proud of it.

Who confesses this kind of thing? I keep pressing down the delete key until these admissions are omitted, but for the love of you and the glory of Christ, I keep them in—right here as we near the end of this journey to a clearer view of amazing grace.

I may be naturally gifted at keeping score, but by the grace of God, I'm becoming a greater score-keeping failure every day.

We can call it lots of things that make sense psychologically, and we can trace some lines around the Enneagram to explain our propensities, but I just want to call it what it is, biblically: keeping score is trying another person in the courtroom of your mind and subjecting them to the law you've declared and the

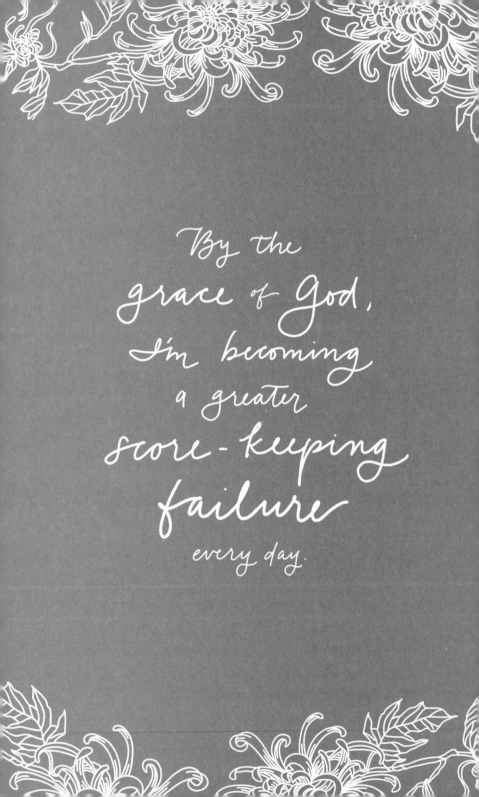

By the
grace of God,
I'm becoming
a greater
score-keeping
failure
every day.

standard you've created. It's counting their missteps and the ways you've covered for them again and again. When we keep score, we play judge and deem who's worthy, who's impossible, who will never change, and who doesn't deserve us. Score keeping says, "Why can't they just be like me?"

It's using words like:

- I deserve . . .
- They should . . .
- I always . . .
- She never . . .

(Please note: I'm not suggesting that we not hold inappropriate, abusive, or destructive relationships accountable. Please seek godly counsel to help you determine the proper response to challenging and hurtful relationships.)

This is about the kind of pride that makes another's sin seem so much worse than my own. This is the kind of pride that believes I've tried everything while others stand by and do nothing. This is the kind of pride that repeats and recounts the wrongs done to me with disgust while dismissing all the ways I've failed others. It's the kind of pride that exists in my nature, which, left unchecked, forgets the very amazing grace that saved a wretch like me.

A wretch like me.

I'm not advocating self-hatred, friends. I'm calling our natural state without Christ what it really is: an ugly, depraved, hopeless mess. But we don't stay coddling our wretchedness. The more we hate our sin and natural state apart from Christ's redemption, the more we'll treasure God's mercy and grace. Paul addressed this by saying, "Wretched man that I am! Who will deliver me from this body of death? Thanks be to God through Jesus Christ our Lord!" (Rom. 7:24–25).

Do you see how this is not a helpless self-diminishing or self-loathing? That's not the path we are called to walk. In fact, would you be surprised to hear that both those self-hating attitudes betray a kind of pride? That's because when we reject grace—God's undeserved favor and forgiveness—and cling to self-hatred instead, we're pridefully holding on to a stubborn idea of what we think we can or cannot be—which, friends, does not take into account the God that made you purposefully.

Self-belittlement and self-loathing actually flow from a heart that excuses itself on account of worthlessness and rejects the hope that is offered. Neither resemble the true humility Paul talked about in Philippians 2:3, a framework for gospel relationships. It's a humility based on the work of grace: "Do nothing from selfish ambition or conceit, but in humility count others more significant than yourselves." The significance of Paul's instruction here is for believers to lay aside the pride that causes us to think ourselves better than others and instead think of others as God does—redeemable, image-bearing souls he's not through with yet.

There's a strong connection between how we treat others and the stories we tell ourselves. And if, as believers, we are to be a part of the body of Christ—the family of God—we must expose the ways we forfeit what God has for us through gospel-centered relationships when we hold on to narratives that are untrue—about ourselves and about others.

True biblical humility looks to grace as our hope in relationships, not how well we can manage our sins or another's to our liking.

Maybe this helps us better discern these attitudes in ourselves:

A graceless narrative sounds like:

- I'm so worthless; I can't believe God loves me at all.
- No one should trust me; I don't even trust myself.
- I'm unlovable.

Self-diminishing says:

- I'm a total mess, it's a wonder anyone trusts me to do anything.
- No one needs my input; I have a bad track record.

In contrast, a grace-informed narrative sounds like:

- Without Christ, I'd be just as capable of lying, deceit, and manipulation.
- By God's grace, I'm not where I hope to be, but I'm sure not where I once was.
- Before I was saved, I only lived for myself. If it didn't please me or feel good, it wasn't worth my time.
- I am so prone to self-centeredness. Without realigning my heart and mind to my true identity in Christ, I'd be self-serving too.

Did you notice how the gracelessness of self-loathing and self-diminishing eventually leads to hopelessness toward others, while the confessional honesty and humility of a biblical self-assessment leads to a response of grace toward the weaknesses of others? Those who keep score with others tend to keep score with themselves. Beating ourselves up for past and present sin when we are redeemed children of God isn't just ineffective, it's contrary to God's forgiveness. This might be a good time to do a self-check:

1. What have you struggled to forgive in yourself?
2. What do you struggle to forgive in others?
3. What do you think you need in order to forgive what you answered in the previous two questions? (Hint: if your answer to this question involves something you can measure in yourself or in someone else, you may be forgetting the benefits of grace.)

It's hard to withhold forgiveness or to fester in bitterness toward someone who has wronged you when you remember the horrendous mess you were and are apart from Christ.

Yes, there are real consequences for past mistakes, dumb choices, and rebellion toward God. But when we surrender all to the saving work of Christ, there is no condemnation for us or for our fellow believers before the cross (Rom. 8:1). God sees us as beloved and unblemished—he sees us as he sees his perfect son, Christ. He chooses to apply grace and call us forgiven because of himself, not because we've proven our worthiness. That's why we can't work to forgive others until we first receive Christ's forgiveness of our own shortcomings.

Grace makes it possible for us to stop trying to fix others and forgive them instead, on account of God's favor when we can't quite muster up our own. Which is to say: forgiveness is a function of living out what we believe, not an act dependent on the way we feel. Grace makes it possible for us to relinquish our control of another's behavior and remember, instead, that God is the author of transformation and change.

Our choosing to forgive others is how we know grace is amazing in our lives. It's honestly one of the most astounding fruits of our salvation. By the grace of God, I don't have to feel good about all the unresolved issues in my family story to forgive the ones who have caused hurt. By the grace of God, I don't have to feel happy about the betrayals and unfair circumstances I've experienced in the past in order to forgive. The more I practice and exercise forgiveness in the everyday moments of my life, the more I realize I'm called to the same humility and forgiveness with all the bigger, hard-to-grasp hurts in my life.

A Soft Heart

A few weeks ago, in the middle of piecing thoughts together for this chapter, I found myself in a heated argument with a family member who was visiting from out of town. What was said and who said what is not as important as why we both felt so angry and upended in this unexpected argument that came out of nowhere. Looking back, it was pretty simple:

1. We all come to any conversation or topic with history, baggage, wounds, and biases.
2. We look to others—especially family—to fill in the holes in our need for encouragement, approval, and affirmation.
3. A record of wrongs against another rears its ugly head

whenever you're feeling attacked unless you actively destroy it.

4. We want the grace or leniency that we're often unwilling to offer another person.

5. We want to be known for what we mean, not how we appear.

These realities stirred a tender pot for both of us and caused things to boil over. And the wounds that resulted from judging each other in response were ultimately worse and more painful than the hurt from the original offense. Don't you love how that happens?

In the moment, my defenses were way up. I was hard-hearted and not backing down. (Ahem, you could say I was absolutely, in no way, grace-laced.) I was not actively thinking thoughts informed by the grace of God, like, *I've been loved and forgiven more than I deserve; I have more than enough love and forgiveness to give.*

No, in the moment, my heart pounded out of my chest like a stone. And with every expression on my face and word from my lips, I worked to declare, "I deserve better from you! How could you misjudge me and speak to me this way? You don't love me! I am *so* disappointed in you."

Of course, I didn't say these words; I didn't have to.

What we want in the midst of keeping score and counting up wrongs is *to win*. But the way of grace is that victory has already been accomplished in all the ways we really need and want. If we no longer have to fight for another's approval for assurance, no longer need applause for motivation, and no longer need another's affirmation in order to know our God-given purpose, then we no longer need to go to battle in order to receive it. Any offense toward us doesn't mar the image of God printed on our souls; our identities are secure in him.

What brings us to forgiveness, repentance, and softness of heart will never be first and foremost a strong argument or a compromise but rather when God's people overflow with the immeasurable kindness of God that led them to repentance in the first place (Rom. 2:4).

By God's grace, we, his children, don't respond out of alignment with the gift we've been given without conviction from the Holy Spirit, who reminds us of what the cross purchased on our behalf. For me, the sting of a sinful response burned in my chest, and—as it is when grace is at work in our lives—my heart softened. I think that's what Paul was talking about in Romans 7 when he confessed that there was a warring between what his flesh wanted to do and what his spirit—saved by grace—was now made to do (vv. 14–25). Our sin-bent hearts may harden this side of heaven, but by God's grace, we don't stay there. Grace softens our hearts to receive salvation but continues to soften our hearts as we return to the fold of God's forgiveness, again and again.

As the Lord Forgave You . . .

What good is grace, and how can it be amazing, if we still have to bring every wrong to justice by our own means?

How many times have you withheld favor from your kids, spouse, friends, or family members, believing that to give them grace is to excuse their behavior? Giving grace, when we are not Jesus, is not pardoning sin or acting as savior. It's simply removing yourself as judge and jury and extending and communicating

That same grace
that pronounced us
forgiven is the
very **grace** we often
withhold when we
choose not to forgive
and allow
bitterness to fester.

the very grace of God that has rescued you from being labeled *hopeless, disappointing, unforgivable.*

That same grace that pronounced us forgiven is the very grace we often withhold when we choose not to forgive and allow bitterness to fester.

That's why Paul the Apostle could write, "Bear with each other and forgive one another if any of you has a grievance against someone. Forgive as the Lord forgave you" (Col. 3:13 NIV).

As the Lord forgave you . . .

Which begs the question: Do we actually consider how much we've been forgiven in Christ on a daily, moment-by-moment basis? If we were to dwell in the wonder of that forgiveness, would there be room to be simultaneously bitter and unable to forgive?

Praise God that we're never far from conflicts or hurts, big and small. I don't even have to leave my house (hello, the year 2020) to have ample opportunities to exercise forgiveness. Forgiveness is a daily opportunity to gauge whether we are actively living into the grace we've been given. We know the work of grace is active and true in our lives when it not only affects the way we see ourselves and others but also causes us to act accordingly.

And so, as those who have been won over by the kindness and patience of God and have tasted of God's grace, we can now take that grace—the grace that moved us from *God is against me* to *God is for me*—and extend it to others.

"For by the grace given to me I say to everyone among you not to think of himself more highly than he ought to think" (Rom. 12:3).

Grace doesn't just make it possible to humble ourselves and forgive; it bids us to, on account of Christ.

FIFTEEN

Grace Is Enough to Hold You Together

Nothing in my hand I bring,
Simply to the cross I cling.
—Augustus Toplady, "Rock of Ages, Cleft for Me"

Sometimes people write books on topics they've mastered. They tell stories that no longer haunt them; they paint pictures they see clearly in their mind's eye. They offer sound counsel on the other side of survival and expertise.

And sometimes, authors invite you on a journey they are still on.

These pages have been the latter.

I wish I could tell you that I don't continue to wrestle with the cultural norms from which I was born and still live within. I wish I could say I always keep my eyes fixed on the eternal citizenship in which my hope lies. I wish I was telling you stories on the other side of making sense of all my history, familial hurts, and questions of belonging. I wish I had perfectly tied-up statements about what it is to be a believer caught between two worlds, in more ways than one.

Some things in your history and mine won't ever be fully understood with clarity this side of heaven.

But I *am* writing to you from the other side of finding the grace of God more than enough to sustain me for all that I have yet to comprehend. I'm no expert, and I've certainly not arrived, but I am standing on the shores of grace, calling out to all those feeling stuck out on the waves to stop treading water and to come to dry land and rest.

Stop the anxious treading and bobbing, and fall on the solid ground of God's amazing grace.

I see you, friend, nodding your head knowingly as I've described the pressures to perform.

I see you, sister, insides turning when you hear of how I've wondered if I'm worthy or loved apart from my ability to exceed expectations. You know. You've been there.

And I see you, believer, confronted with how you've trusted God's grace to save you but haven't truly believed it can transform you.

I promise: You're not behind. You're not too late. You're joining me here on this shore, right on time.

This book is for you, right where you are.

The grace of God deserves an ocean of words and a millennium's worth of excavating its depths and wonders. These chapters are but the tip of the iceberg, the first ray of the sunrise, the first unfurling petal of a garden rose in bloom. This is my finite telling of the story of the infinite abundance that's found in the gift of God's grace through Jesus.

I beg you, friend, take your eyes off of everything you think you need to be amazing, and be amazed, instead, at God's grace. Square your shoulders and fully turn your heart's longings and desire to know and be known to him. Don't settle for a peripheral glance now and then. Don't be content to grow numb to this extravagant gift. Let us not be among those amazed by ourselves and unimpressed with grace that we call "amazing."

Remember, we have the gift that generations longed to know fully. What was hidden to others before us is now ours. We have no good reason to return to the chains of self-improvement and self-striving. We know better because we've been given better.

> The mystery hidden for ages and generations but now revealed to his saints. To them God chose to make known how great among the Gentiles are the riches of the glory of this mystery, which is Christ in you, the hope of glory. Him we proclaim, warning everyone and teaching everyone with all wisdom, that we may present everyone mature in Christ. For this I toil, struggling with all his energy that he powerfully works within me. (Col. 1:26–29)

Paul felt urgency as he wrote to the Colossians, and I come to you with this same desire that you be steadfast in the truth, unwavering and not lamed by the shifting winds of self-fulfillment.

The one thing I want you to know, more than anything else, is that if you are truly in Christ, you can stop trying so hard to be who

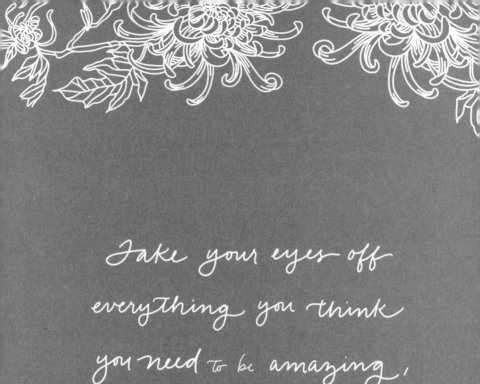

Take your eyes off everything you think you need to be amazing, and **be** amazed, instead, at *God's grace.*

you already are in Jesus. The riches of his glory equate to Christ in you. This is not of your own doing; it is the gift of God!

This alone makes you enough before the throne of God. This alone enables you to be more than you could strive to be on your own.

On our last day, whether that is today or twenty years from now, when we meet Jesus face-to-face, I want both of us—you and me, friend—to be in the presence of our God, mature in Christ. That's the end goal of every word that's been written here and every story told—that we might live into everything that God purposes for us as grace-made daughters of God.

How do I know we can stand mature, held fast and secure, made pure and blameless before a God who deserves and demands so much more than we can give? Because we stand on the grace that delivers this kind of assurance:

> For the grace of God has appeared, bringing salvation for all people, training us to renounce ungodliness and worldly passions, and to live self-controlled, upright, and godly lives in the present age, waiting for our blessed hope, the appearing of the glory of our great God and Savior Jesus Christ, who gave himself for us to redeem us from all lawlessness and to purify for himself a people for his own possession who are zealous for good works. (Titus 2:11–14)

Paul summed it up for us, friend. He said it better than I ever could. God's grace saves, trains, purifies, and sustains. And most of all, God's grace makes us his. Even the good works and the fire inside to go after them is *by grace*.

At the end of our days, when we cross over into glory, we'll have questions that won't seem to matter anymore, and earthly sorrow will pass away. But we won't bring along our resumes, and that stunning career accomplishment will look dingy against the white-hot glory of God's holiness. The number of boxes you checked off next to your Bible reading plan won't be your badge; the seal of the Holy Spirit on a surrendered heart will tell of your arrival. And in the presence of our Holy God, what will keep us from incinerating on the spot will be our safekeeping in the cleft of the Rock—the covering of grace through the blood of Christ— that shelters us now and holds us fast into eternity.

I know you think you have to hold it all together—your home, your kids, your school schedule, your relationships, your family dynamics, your work performance, your fears, and your pursuit of God.

But the life-transforming gospel of grace declares that it is Christ who is holding all things together. He's the one who holds you secure in the arms of grace. So, you can rest, friend. You really can. Not a forgetful, complacent rest but a deep and unhindered surrender. It's a rest that brings to a halt our endless well digging and causes us to lay down our shovels for good, in exchange for a cup to drink from. It's the rest that makes these familiar words actually true:

> *Not the labors of my hands*
> *Can fulfill thy law's demands;*
> *Could my zeal no respite know,*
> *Could my tears forever flow,*
> *All for sin could not atone;*
> *Thou must save, and thou alone.*
> *Nothing in my hand I bring,*

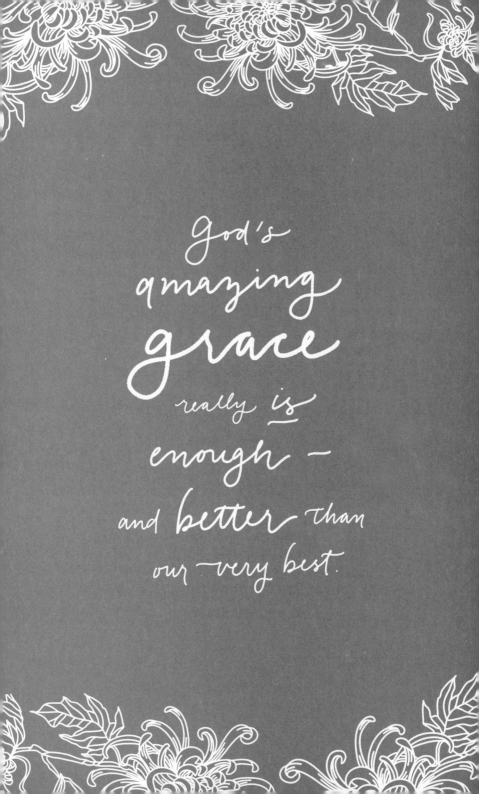

God's
amazing
grace
really *is*
enough —
and **better** than
our very best.

Simply to the cross I cling;
Naked, come to thee for dress;
Helpless, look to thee for grace;
Foul, I to the fountain fly;
Wash me, Savior, or I die.[1]

It's here, where the helpless like you and me, in need of grace, find true respite for our striving, until the day of Christ. Not relying on our own agility or resilience, we are the ones who bend and bow low—but are not easily broken. We are the ones who stand firm on the grace of God.

So when do strivings cease?

Strivings cease when . . .

. . . we no longer need to prove our worth.
. . . we stop chasing approval as our comfort.
. . . we glory in our weaknesses.
. . . God is greater than our accomplishments.
. . . we know peace apart from pleasing others.
. . . God is for us and no longer against us.
. . . Jesus so captures our gaze we stop chasing everything
*   else.*[2]

So, I invite you, friend, to cling to the mercies of God while he never lets you go—right here, where grace abounds and strivings cease.

God's amazing grace really *is* enough—and better than our very best.

A Closing Prayer

O Lord,
May I never fail to come to the knowledge of the truth,
never rest in a system of doctrine, however
scriptural, that does not bring or further salvation,
or teach me to deny ungodliness and worldly lusts,
or help me to live soberly, righteously, godly;
never rely on my own conditions and resolutions,
but be strong in thee and in thy might;
never cease to find thy grace sufficient
in all my duties, trials, and conflicts;
never forget to repair to thee
in all my spiritual distresses and outward troubles,
in all the dissatisfactions experienced in creature comforts;
never fail to retreat to him who is full of grace and truth,
the friend that loveth at all times,
who is touched with feelings of my infirmities,
and can do exceeding abundantly for me;
never confine my religion to extraordinary occasions,
but acknowledge thee in all my ways;
never limit my devotions to particular seasons

but be in thy fear all the day long;
never be godly only on the sabbath or in thy house,
but on every day abroad and at home;
never make piety a dress but a habit,
not only a habit but a nature,
not only a nature but a life.
Do good to me by all thy dispensations,
by all means of grace,
by worship, prayers, praises,
And at last let me enter that world where is no temple,
but only thy glory and the Lamb's.

—ARTHUR BENNETT, FROM *THE VALLEY OF VISION*

Acknowledgments

This book literally would not exist without, and apart from, the grace of God. May you, Father, be honored and gloried in these pages.

One hundred percent of this book was written in the middle of 2020's global pandemic, which means that my home base—my family of eight—witnessed every bit of this process and loved me through this intense labor of love.

Troy, you're my best friend, my trusted counselor, my nearest confidante, and the shepherd of our home and my ministry. You've lived and preached this message of grace in my life more than any other.

Caleb, Liam, Judah, Stone, Asa, and Haddon: Thank you, boys, for being my biggest defenders and loudest cheering section. You've sacrificed, supported, and picked up the slack. You've made meals, cared for one another, and filled this home with laughter; I couldn't do any of this without you (or the Topo Chicos you deliver).

To Bill Jensen, I'll always be grateful for this significant season and your partnership that made this book possible. You read these words first—and nothing put wind in my sail more than your response to my early manuscript: "This book is about God." Bill, your love for Jesus makes me want to know him more, and I'm so grateful for the partnership we've had in this season.

Jenni Burke, thank you for the support you've extended to me as we begin a new relationship together. Your care and investment in my journey is a gift to me.

Ruth Samsel, thanks for listening to my stories in 2015 and planting the seed that eventually became this book.

To my editor-turned-friend, Jessica Wong Rogers: God was so kind to bring us together. I smile when I think of all the conversations we've had through the journey of this book. And all the amazing food, dreamt about and shared. What a blessing, through and through. Your belief in this message gave me courage.

To my team at Nelson Books—especially Tim Paulson, Brigitta Nortker, Jennifer Gingerich, and Kristen Golden—thank you for championing this message and for your dedicated support. Your energy, attention to detail, and care for me have sustained and bolstered me in this season!

And to Sara, Ashley, and Eve—my core curriculum team—thank you for loving the word of God and the clarity of the gospel. So grateful to bring this study to women, together.

To my GraceLaced team—Sarah, Gina, Camille, Kenzie, Ana, Eve, Jamie, and Rachael. I couldn't ask for a more dedicated group of sisters to create, serve, and walk with. You make it possible (and a joy) for me to be faithful right where I am.

Sarah Alexander, thank you for being my creative and artistic partner, and for growing with me artistically year by year. I can't believe all that we've been able to create together.

Eve Stipes, thank you for lending your heart and your friendship to the processing of these pages. Who knew we'd (still) get to do ministry together after all these years. To Caleb Peavy and the Unmutable team, thank you for cheering on this message to the finish line yet again.

Josh Lewis, thank you for the more-than-I-can-carry stack of books from your library, which were invaluable to the research and preparation for this book. Your care and prayers for me and our family have been life giving.

Vivian and Jamie, thank you for the sisterhood that has become such a balm as I found a voice for my Asian American journey. That first podcast episode and that first time speaking to the Someday Is Here community were significant milestones of discovery for me—thank you for your friendship and welcome.

To my Mama and Baba, your life lessons have become part of my own. Because of grace, we get to keep growing; God's not through with us yet.

When a book is forty-six years in the making, there are more people to thank than can fit on these pages. The Lord has used so many to teach and show me the grace of God. This book is the fruit of their faithfulness to preach, speak, live, and demonstrate: by grace, alone.

For from him and through him and to him are all things.
—ROMANS 11:36

Notes

Introduction

1. G. K. Chesterton, *What's Wrong with the World* (Hollywood, FL: Simon & Brown, 2018).

Chapter 4: The Welcome We Long For

1. *Mise En Place*, episode 4, "How a Master Chef Built a Michelin-Starred Taiwanese Restaurant in a Strip Mall," directed by Daniel Geneen, featuring Chef Jon Yao, video shared April 4, 2020, by Eater, on YouTube, 13:59, https://www.youtube.com/watch?v=NGbFtTYQpus&ab_channel=Eater.

2. *Mise En Place*, 0:54.

Chapter 5: Pressure to Perform

1. *Chariots of Fire*, directed by Hugh Hudson (London: Warner Bros. Pictures, 1981).

2. Clay Skipper, "Why Self-Help Might Actually Be Making You Less Happy," *GQ*, September 5, 2018, https://www.gq.com/story/why-self-help-makes-you-less-happy.

Chapter 6: The Lunchroom

1. Anne Lamott, *Bird by Bird* (New York: Pantheon Books, 1994; New York: Anchor Books, 1995), 32–33.

2. Brené Brown, *Daring Greatly: How the Courage to Be Vulnerable Transforms the Way We Live, Love, Parent, and Lead* (Los Angeles: Gotham Books, 2012; New York: Avery, 2015), 145–46.

3. "Heidelberg Catechism: Introduction," trans. Faith Alive Christian Resources, Christian Reformed Church, 2011, https://www.crcna.org/welcome/beliefs/confessions/heidelberg-catechism.

Chapter 7: Honor and Shame

1. Curt Thompson, *The Soul of Shame: Retelling the Stories We Believe About Ourselves* (Downers Grove, IL: InterVarsity Press, 2015), 24.

2. Abdu Murray, "Canceled: How the Eastern Honor-Shame Mentality Traveled West," The Gospel Coalition, May 28, 2020, https://www.thegospelcoalition.org/article/canceled-understanding-eastern-honor-shame/.

3. Tim Keller, "The Two Prodigal Sons: Reading & Reflection," sermon shared by Campus Outreach Minneapolis, http://www.cominneapolis.org/s/The-Two-Prodigal-Sons-Reading-Reflection-by-Tim-Keller.pdf.

4. Edward T. Welch, *Shame Interrupted* (Greensboro, NC: New Growth Press, 2012), 107.
5. Insights derived from multiple sources influenced by Kenneth Bailey's studies of the Middle East and from biblical stories.
6. Keller, "The Two Prodigal Sons: Reading & Reflection."

Chapter 9: Grace Makes New, Not Better

1. John F. MacArthur, *The Gospel According to the Apostles* (Nashville: Thomas Nelson, 2000), 47.
2. Matt Chandler, *The Explicit Gospel* (Wheaton, IL: Crossway, 2012), 199.
3. MacArthur, *Gospel According to the Apostles*, 25.
4. Dietrich Bonhoeffer, *The Cost of Discipleship* (New York: Simon & Schuster, 1995), 43, 45.
5. Jerry Bridges, *The Discipline of Grace: God's Role and Our Role in the Pursuit of Holiness* (Colorado Springs: NavPress, 2006), 19.

Chapter 11: Grace Cancels Our Debt, For Real

1. Lauren Mack, "The Significance of Red Envelopes in Chinese Culture," ThoughtCo, August 17, 2019, https://www.thoughtco.com/chinese-new-year-red-envelope-687537.
2. Jerry Bridges, *The Discipline of Grace: God's Role and Our Role in the Pursuit of Holiness* (Colorado Springs: NavPress, 2006), 111.
3. John Piper, *Future Grace* (Colorado Springs: Multnomah Books, 2012), 30.
4. Julia H. Johnston, "Marvelous Grace of Our Loving Lord," written in 1910, hymn number 120 in *One Lord, One Faith, One Baptism* (Chicago: GIA Publications, 2018), Hymnary.org, https://hymnary.org/text/marvelous_grace_of_our_loving_lord.
5. *Westminster Shorter Catechism*, "Question 1," Westminster Shorter Catechism Project, Bible Presbyterian Church, last updated May 21, 2019, https://www.shortercatechism.com/resources/wsc/wsc_001.html.

Chapter 13: Grace Replaces Fear with Freedom

1. Jerry Bridges, *The Discipline of Grace: God's Role and Our Role in the Pursuit of Holiness* (Colorado Springs: NavPress, 2006), 232–33.
2. J. D. Greear, "Satan's Go-To Temptation Against You," Desiring God, August 3, 2018, https://www.desiringgod.org/articles/satans-go-to-temptation-against-you.
3. Jennie Allen, *Get Out of Your Head: Stopping the Spiral of Toxic Thoughts* (Colorado Springs: WaterBrook, 2020), 61.
4. Sinclair Ferguson, *By Grace Alone: How the Grace of God Amazes Me* (Lake Mary, FL: Reformation Trust Publishers, 2010), 76.
5. Charles Wesley, "And Can It Be That I Should Gain," written in 1738, hymn number 307 in *Sing Joyfully* (Carol Stream, IL: Tabernacle Publications, 1989), Hymnary.org, https://hymnary.org/text/and_can_it_be_that_i_should_gain.

Chapter 15: Grace Is Enough to Hold You Together

1. Augustus Toplady "Rock of Ages, Cleft for Me," written in 1776, hymn number 361 in *United Methodist Hymnal* (Nashville, TN: United Methodist Publishing House, 1989), Hymnary.org, https://hymnary.org/text/rock_of_ages_cleft_for_me_let_me_hide.
2. In order listed: 2 Thessalonians 1:11; 1 John 4:4; 2 Corinthians 12:9; Psalm 145:3; Colossians 1:20; Romans 8:31; Psalm 73:25.

About the Author

RUTH CHOU SIMONS is a *Wall Street Journal* bestselling and award-winning author of several books, including *GraceLaced*, *Beholding and Becoming*, and *Foundations*. Her first Bible study curriculum, *TruthFilled*, released in 2020. She is an artist, entrepreneur, and speaker who uses each of these platforms to spiritually sow the Word of God into people's hearts. Through her online shoppe at GraceLaced.com and her social media community, Simons shares her journey of God's grace intersecting daily life with word and art. Ruth and her husband, Troy, are grateful parents to six boys—their greatest adventure.

New Video Study for Your Church or Small Group

If you've enjoyed this book, now you can go deeper with the companion video Bible study!

In this six-session study, Ruth Chou Simons helps you apply the principles in *When Stivings Cease* to your life. The study guide includes streaming video access, video teaching notes, group discussion questions, personal reflection questions, and a leader's guide.

Study Guide plus
Streaming Video
9780310130048

DVD
9780310130062

Available now at your favorite bookstore,
or streaming video on StudyGateway.com.